T0368357

This Book Is Dedicated
To Three Of The Evocative Muses
Meena Naomi Chudasama
Sabina Marliza Donnelly
Claire Leigh Griffiths
That Have Personified
An' Presided Over The Sources
Of Inspiration & The Genius Symbolized
Within The Literary Sparks
Of The Jibba Jabba Bird.

JIBBA JABBA
The
B I R D

जबि्बा.१ॐ१ जब्बा.ॐ१ पक्षी.ॐॡ

Clive Alando Taylor

authorHOUSE®

AuthorHouse™ UK
1663 Liberty Drive
Bloomington, IN 47403 USA
www.authorhouse.co.uk
Phone: UK TFN: 0800 0148641 (Toll Free inside the UK)
*   UK Local: (02) 0369 56322 (+44 20 3695 6322 from outside the UK)*

Published by AuthorHouse 12/27/2023

ISBN: 979-8-8230-8544-1 (sc)
ISBN: 979-8-8230-8545-8 (e)

Library of Congress Control Number: 2023921655

Print information available on the last page.

This book is printed on acid-free paper.

1. एकम्.ኣንድ

SONGVERSATION

जब्बा.የጅባ जब्बा.ጀባ पक्षी.ወፍ

A PROSPEROUS BOOK

♧♤♧

By The Age Of Fourteen

I'd Already Seen

A Formation Of Stars

In Receipt Of A Dream

As The Soberin' Thoughts

Entered My Mind

Collidin' Inside

As They Opened My Eyes

It Spoke An' It Told

Of An' Endless War

Across All The Ages

Centuries Old

But Nobody Knew

What They Were Fightin' For

The Strong An' The Weak

The Rich An' The Poor

In The Pantheon

Of My Retail

The Words Came

Fallin' Down

Like A Fairytale

Like A Coveted Prize

That I Would Come To Inherit

I Tore It Up

To Start All Over Again

An' As I Looked Inside

I Was Surely Hooked

Beyond The Grotesque

An' The Beautiful

An' As The Secret Was Found

That I Undertook

It Was All Bound Up

Like A Prosperous Book. ☆

THE FUTURE
(OUT OF TIME)

There Is A Force, It Lives Inside
Sometimes You Find It In Humankind

Its' Always Bein' There Come Rain Or Shine
Its' Always In U're Dreams An' A Will To Survive

When Somethin' So Heavy, Is Weighin' On U're Mind
An' You Often Wonda' Will I Live Or Die

An' The War That Rages Deepa' Down Inside
Is The Battle That You Fight From The Left To The Right

Is There Anythin' Left To Make You Realize
Now That U're Holdin' The Keys To The Rest Of U're Life

Now That The Time Has Come For You To Decide
Before We Finally Pay The Ultimate Price

The Bet Is Always On The Future
An' Yet Its' Always One Second To Midnight

The Bet is Always On The Future
Now That It Seems We're Out Of Time. ☆

U'RE LIFE

It All Begins
At The Very End
The Last Breath
May Be U're First
Or Could It Be
That U've Lived An' Died
Somehow Goin' Forwards
In Reverse
U're Memories
Hold The Key
Like A Movin' Picture
Inside Of U're Mind
Through The Perceptions
Of U're Sensories
Jus' As You Remember
How Far U've Come
U're Emotions
Are Jus' Like The Sea
Through A Myriad
A Place So Volatile
Sailin' Upon
That Endless Journey
Takin' A Step
One Day At A Time

Reality Is A Victory
      For All That You See
            Livin' Inside
                  Somehow It Shows
                        What U've Always Known
                              What It Always Feels Like
                              For The First Time
                                    U're Gonna Wake Up
                        In A Dream
                  Somewhere Between
            Day An' Night
      No Matta' The Things
   You Have Seen
Or The Places U've Bein
In U're Life. ☆

THE WORLD

♣♠♣

You Can't Have A King
Without A Queen
When All That It Seems
Is Good Will Hunting
Her Loyalty Is Royalty
Its' Tit For Tat, Yeah
Whatever You Put In
Is What You Get Back
There Was Always One
Said It Could Never Be Done
A Beast Of Burden
Underneath Your Thumb
Now Ya' Know How It Feels
To Be Denied
What You Could Never Behold
What You Could Never Have
Don't You Know That Heaven
Is Someone Else's Hell
Yeah For One To Win
One Has To Lose As Well
So Be Careful
What U're Wishing For
B'cos You Might Just Get
Everything You Want

I Came Through The Door
Rough, Rugged And Raw
Just To Rob From The Rich
Just To Feed Poor
Now Were Standing On The Edge
Of Brinkmanship
So Turn Out The Lights
The First One To Blink
An Eye For An Eye
A Tooth For A Tooth
A Knife For A Gun
For A Ghetto Youth
Not A War Of Violence
Just A War Of Silence
Not A War Of Weapons
Just A War That Deafens
When The People In The Front
Have To Face The Facts
Now You Do A U-Turn
Re-Check And Look Back
We Shouldn't Just Survive
Just To Stay Alive
To Continue To Strive
As We Learn To Thrive
Now U're Following The Paths
Laid Out For You
Well Its' Gotta Be True, Inevitable

You Can Walk With Me
Instead Of Stalking Me
As The Walls Fall Away
With The Sky Set Free
How The People On The Top
Topple Down Like That
I Beg You Pass Me The Ball
In A Game Of Catch
In A Game Of 2 Halves
Were A Perfect Match
Now The Earth Is Shaking
The Earth Is Quaking
With Too Much Blood
Spilling From Creation
Whoever Said The Deal Is Real
Whoever Said The World Is Square
Whoever Said The World Is Equal
Just Might Not Be So Fair
Yeah B.C.E
Before The Common Era
A.D-Anno Domini
The Year Of Our Lord
As We Advance The Ages
Of Another Phenomena
Another Metaphor
Seems To Strikes A Chord

With The Ears To Hear
And The Eyes To See
Predicate This Rhyme's
Not Just Poetry
From The Richest Wisdom
To The Poorest Needs
Still Dividing Up The Portions Equally
From Left To Right
From Front To Back
With The Cherub And The Lion
And The Eagle And The Ox
Read Chapter And Verse
To Reverse The Curse
Before You Wind Up
Dead In A Hearse
For What Goes Around
Keeps Coming Around
And Whatever Goes Up
Must Come Down
Like Sex n' Drugs n' Rock n' Roll
Is The Quickest Way
To Empty Out Ya' Soul
Now U're Cup Is Empty
Watch It Overflow
From The Skies Above
And The Earth Below

Innocent Or Shyness
U're Royal Highness
Commit To The Random Acts
Of All Kindness
Its' Never Really Over
Its' Only Set Aside
If There's Any Other Way
You Know We Woulda' Tried
From The Kitchen Sink
To The Xtra Mile
I Give 100%
Followed By The Whole 9
Ich Me Sun Chi
Each One Teach One
Proverbs Must Be
Easy Go Easy Come
Before You Learn To Speak
You Better Learn What To Say
In A Decadent Way
A Decade Of Decay
Or Could It Be That The Liberty
Gives Another False Sense Of Security
B'coz The Muse Is Lying
The Muse Is Crying
The Muse Is Death
And The Muse Is Dying

Forget The Small Talk
And Check The Conditions
If U're Chuntering From
A Sedentary Position
Yeah United We Stand
And Divided We Fall
And So On, And So On
And So Forth
Weighing Up The Options
Still Weighing Me Down
Tying Up The Loose Ends
Before I Move On Out
Still Carrying The Cross
Of The Carrion Crow
To Have Possession
And Still Lose Control
In A Battle Of The Sexes
A Complex Nexus
What Race Is To Colour
With The Prejudices
As We Hope For The Best
And Prepare For The Worst
As A Second Opinion
Is To Second Guess
So Don't Be Amazed
At The Amount Of Praise
For The Desired Effect
To Reconnect

As I Did The Time
In The Prison Of My Mind
Now Its' Time For You
To Free My Life
We Don't Live To Eat
We Just Eat To Live
Because Everybody Dies
But Not Everybody Lives
The World Is Jus' A Circle
It Jus' Goes Round And Round
U're Born, Until Die
Then You End Up In The Ground
The Closer You Get To God
The Closer The Devil Will Get To You
Its' Jus' A Struggle For Ya' Soul
There's Nothing More That You Can Do
Until U're Resurrected
Or Maybe Not Nobody Knows
But As Far As I Can Tell
That's The Way The Story Goes. ☆

BROKEN HEART

I Think It Was Mo'

Than 10 Years Ago

I Was The Brightest Spark

But Now I'm A Zero

It Was Spose' To Be

The Greatest Day Of My Life

But Sumpthin' From The Past

Left Me Payin' The Price

When I Was Young

This Was The Biggest Town

An' Life Was So Surreal

An' It Was So Profound

An' In That Church

On The Corner

The Preacher Held Me Down

But That Was Then

An' This Is Now

On The Day That I Lost

She Was Precious To Me

I Was A Saplin' Flower

She Was A Peachy Tree

I Had The World In My Sights

I Was So Full Of Dreams

But My Virginity

Was Never No Sweet 16

An' Now Those Scars

From The Past

Have Left Their Mark

An' All This Time I Was Workin'

With A Broken Heart

Livin' On Borrowed Time

Right From The Start

An' Those Forget-Me-Nots

Of A Broken Heart. ☆

CLOSER TO HEAVEN
(BABY)

Baby I'm Walkin' The Line
Goin' Back An' Forth Until You Surrender

Baby You Are The One
The Only One I Want, Lovin' Me Tenda'

Baby Jus' Gimme U're Best
B'Cos I Know We Can Do Betta'

Baby We're Up Against The Rest
An' I Know We Got To Keep It Together

Cos I Bein' Waitin All This Time
Jus' For You To Let It Show

An' I Will Do What It Takes
To Make You Mine Before We Stop An' Go

Baby We Got To Make It Straight
Instead Of Goin' Roun' in Circles

Baby We Got To Take It There
Not Even For A Day, But Now An' Forever

We Got A Long Way To Go
So Give Me U're All, Its' Not Too Far To Fall

An' When You Hear That Beckon Call
We Can Move Closer, Closer To Heaven. ☆

GOOD ADVICE

Anotha' T.V Station

Brainwashin' The Nation

The Reasons For U're Pain An' Insanity

He Never Got What He Came For

All The Things That We Paid For

Now There's Bodies Scattered

All Over The Floor

Well Ain't It Funny They Say

The Boy Was Actin' Strange

Nothin' Short Of Deranged

When The Damage Was Done

Cos Everybody He Turn Too

Misunderstood

What He Went Through

An' Nobody Listened

As He Suffered Them All

Its' Not So Easy You See

To Be Livin' Scot Free

With A Billion Trillion Images

Inside Of U're Mind

Maybe He Figured Them Out

What They Were Talkin' About

Some Call It Paranoia

But Its' Hard To Define

Maybe God Is Tryin'

To Help You

Out Of U're Mess

The Same Kinda' Mess

The Devil Got You Into

But It Seems We Pay The Price

For Some Good Advice

That Might Jus' Cost You

Mo' Than U're Life. ☆

ITS' ALL ABOUT

♧♤♧

Do You Know The Story Of Mankind
Cos There Is Somethin' So Heavy
Weighin' On My Mind
What's Lived In The Past
Is Never Left Behind
It Seems We Repeat
The Same Story All The Time
We Always Say What We Want
We Always Say What We Need
From This Relationship
But We Can Hardly Agree
Actin' So Selfishly Jus' To Preserve
The Point Of Our Pride
We Forget What Its' Worth
Spendin' Time Together
Til' We End Up Apart
Jus' To Apologise
For Breakin' U're Heart
But Love Is Never Love
Until Its' Come An' Gone
How Could Somethin' So Right
End Up So Wrong
Its' All About Love, Its' All About Hello
Its' All About Goodbye, I'm Lettin' You Go
Its' All About You, Its' All About Me
Its' All About The Need, To Be Free. ☆

LONELY YEARS

♣♠♣

I Was Born Upon
　That Fateful Day

　　The One Where Lovers
　　　Give Their Hearts Away

　　　　Jus' Like Mistletoe
　　　　　Their Only Wish

　　　　　　Is To Kiss You With
　　　　　　　Hollywood Lips

Its' Not A Golden Rule
　That You Learn In School

　　While You Go Diggin' An' Searchin'
　　　For Somethin' Beautiful

　　　　Now That U're Soul Is Exposed
　　　　　In The Emperor's New Clothes

　　　　　　An' You End Up Wearin'
　　　　　　　Nothin' But The Truth

Its' The Only Gift
    That You Get For Free

        Its' The Only Gift
            You Give To Anybody

                Its' The Only Thing
                    That You Can Choose

                        When There's Nothin' Left
                        For You To Lose

This Is A Story
    Full Of Hopes An' Fears

        Written By Me
            In My Lonely Years

                Its' Not Jus' A Fate
                  You Can Escape

                      As Destiny Waits
                        In Those Lonely Years. ☆

MAKES US HUMAN

Its' Hard To See Beyond This Grief
Ever Since The Day You Took U're Love Away
Though The Wiles Of The Devil May Trick An' Deceive
I Know This Battle I Fight Is Not Won So Easily

If The Afterlife Of Paradise
Is A Deconstruction Of Reality
Where The Beautiful Eyes Of A Frightened Child
Are Filled With Tears Of Such Vanity

I Hoped This Food For Thought Could Make You Whole
Jus' Like Manna To U're Soul
For What Heaven Said Is Written In Red
As We Pay Our Respects Religiously

Though We Live An' Die A Thousand Times
Knowin' This Resurrection Is Our Only Prize
For All The Sovereignty That We Had
These Dominions Of Love Always Brought Us Back

For Now There Never Seems To Be Enough
Somethin' To Fill You Up As Bold As Love
As We Take This Path In Search Of Perfection
Makin' Mistakes Is What Makes Us Human. ☆

ITS' ALL OVER

♣♤♣

Heard Her On The Broadcast

Up Inside The Ether

Transmittin' On A Satellite

With Anotha' Double Agent

I'm Braced' For The Impact

Breakin' Bread For My Wishes

I'm Swimmin' In The Rain

In A State Of Indecision

A Shift In The Paradigm

A Triple Whammy Cross Over

I'm Prayin' By The Riverside

Waitin' On Jehovah

You Can't Choose What You Want

You Can't Lose With A Loser

For All The Saviours In This World

Remember One Had To Suffer

If It Wasn't For The Money

If It Wasn't For The Fame

If It Wasn't For The Imperfections

They'd Treat Us All The Same

Nuthin' To Exchange

For This Immortal Life

Nuthin' To Be Gained

When The Villain Is In U're Mind

Tell Dr Manhattan

I'm Workin For The Martians

Tell Superman

I'm Jus' Anotha' Kryptonian

B'cos I Know You Can't Tell Me Why

By The Look In Her Eyes Its' All Over. ☆

TREE

♣♤♣

If You Wanna Change The World
　　Betta' Start With U'reself
　　　　Gotta Lead By Example
　　　　　　Take It Some Place Else

You Got A Bad Attitude
　　The Impositions Of U're Will
　　　　Jus' Like U're Opinions
　　　　　　Betta' Keep It To U'reself

Could It Be That God
　　Is Helpin' Those Who Help Themselves
　　　　With All This Robbin' An' Lootin'
　　　　　　He' Mus' Be Helpin' Someone Else

If Its' Good Enough For Pah'
　　Then Its' Good Enough For Me
　　　　If Its' Good Enough Mah'
　　　　　　Raisin' Up This Family
　　　　　　　　Choppin' Down That Tree

Gonna Tell You Everythin'
　　Everythin' I Know
　　　　Gonna Put It All Out There
　　　　　　Gonna Put It Up For Sho'. ☆

BEST INTENTIONS

Before You Walk Through The Door

You Know You Walked Through Before

You Know U've Got To Be Right

You Know U've Got To Be Sure

Before You Meet Someone Else

Jus' Do Some Work On U'reself

Then Maybe You Might Get

All The Love You Deserve

You Got To Know The Levels

When The Vibrations Tremble

You Got To Know How The Devil

Is Messin' With U're Plans

Whatever You Believe

You Got To Want What You Need

You Got Try An' Seize it

With Both Hands

You Got To Be Complete

To Sweep Her Off Her Feet

Before You Get The Chance

Of Dancin' Cheek To Cheek

You Got To Let Her Know

Without Removin' Her Clothes

Its' All About The Heart

Mind, Body An' Soul

You Got To Be

Enough For U'reself

Before You Get To The Point

Of Lovin' Somebody Else

Sometimes Our Feelins' Are Exposed

Before Our Best Intentions

Ever Become Known. ☆

PARADISE KNOWS
(COFFEE CUP)

♣♠♣

When I Think
Of Loves Innocence
We Used It All Up
Come Drink My Coffee Cup

Whenever We Thought
It Was Never Enough
I Guess We Spent Too Much
Come Drink My Coffee Cup

The Closer We Got
We Kept On Losing Touch
Runnin' Out Of Luck
Come Drink My Coffee Cup

More Than We Could Know
About This Beautiful Stuff
We Wanted Too Much
Come Drink My Coffee Cup

An' All The Times
We Felt Like Giving Up
I Guess We Couldn't Stop
Come Drink My Coffee Cup

Sometimes It Was Smooth
Sometimes It Was Rough
Through The Hard An' The Soft
Come Drink My Coffee Cup

How Did We Know,
Letting Go
One Door Would Open
But Another Would Close

An' All Of The Highs
An' All Of The Lows
Baby We Took The Blows
Paradise Knows. ☆

BOURGEOISIE

♣♠♣

Evidently Its' All Inevitable

Why You Surrendered All

For Something So Cynical

An' Every Day

U're Dying On U're Feet

Triumphant In U're Battles

Before You Suffer Defeat

Oil, Water An' Blood

Never Seem To Mix

Maybe U're Good Luck

Can Get You Out This Fix

Jus' Like Chalk An' Cheese

We Agree To Disagree

That's Why You Put U're Friends

Before U're Family

I Guess In Personal Terms

We're Fightin' The Same Fight

But Somehow We Ignore

To Put This World To Rights

U're Remotely Alone

But We're Jus' On Our Own

Tryin' To Figure Out

The Darkness From The Light

An' A Voice Of Sedition

With Proverbial Plans

An' Ragin' In The Streets

The Devil's Dressed In Drag

Its' An Insurrection

To Make A Petition

Its' A Commentary

For The Bourgeoisie. ☆

FREEDOM

I Guess My Work Is Done
    An' Yes I Had My Fun

I Got No Reasons To Go
    An' Less Reasons To Stay

I Guess I've Done My Time
    Rewritin' Every Line

Watchin' As The Seasons
    Pass Me By

For Those Without
    A Reason To Live

Maybe You Should Try
    Livin' Off The Grid

For Those Who Wonda'
    If God Would Ever Come

Maybe You Should Try
    Lookin' At The Sun

On A Natural High
    Is How I Survive

Is There Any Other Way
   To Get Through Life

I Got No Bones To Pick
   Ain't Got No 7 Year Itch

I Know They're Diggin' A Ditch
   To Put Me Inside

I'm Disconnected
   From All My Connections

I'm Disassociated
   From My Associations

I'm Disengagin'
   From All My Engagements

I'm Cuttin The Ties
   That I've Bein' Tied Too. ☆

EVERYBODY

♣♠♣

I Bein' Waitin' On The Mailman

To Bring A Letter To Me

Readin' All The Lines

Of U're Poetry

Like A Mother To A Baby

Its' Jus' Human Nature

I'd Like To Pollinate The Flowers

Like A Honey Bee

When There's Shadows In The Night

Take A Shot In The Dark

We Can Light Up The Streets

An' Take A Walk In The Park

Whatever We Forget

Remember What's True

On A Saturday Night

Til Sunday Afternoon

Me An' You

All That We Can Do

Right All The Wrong Things

Make Em' New

Me An' You

We Got To See It Through

Take All The Bad Things

Make Em' Good

Everybody's Walkin'

Away From Love

Everybody Is Sayin'

There's No Way For Love

Everybody Is Waitin'

On That Prayer For Love

Everybody Has Simply

Strayed Away From Love. ☆

THE TRUTH
(APPALLIN' VISTA)

We Don't Care If You Treat Us Like Rejects

Cos All The Things You Do, We No Longer Respec'

We're Not Afraid Of U're Reset

We're Jus' Upset B'Cos You Treat Us Like Objects

We Don't Care If Its' Taken Out Of Context

We're Already Aware Its' Not A New Concept

We're Not Tryin' To Be The Best

But We're Good At What We Do

We Don't Want Promises

We Jus' Want The Truth

Lookin' Through The Lens Of An' Appallin' Vista

An' What Seems To Be Goin' Down The Tube

It Might Be A Process Of Elimination

Although U're Attitude Is Not Our Point Of View. ☆

ANOTHA' SPECIES

♣♤♣

Computations Of Variants
U're Name, U're Sex An' U're Age

Survival Of The Fittest
To Adapt An' Change

A Supernatural World
Extraordinary Beings

Full Of Hyper Intelligence
Invadin' All Of Our Dreams

U're Genesis Arises
U're Genealogy

To Procreate An' Activate
Anotha' Pedigree

This Is Life Of A Physical Manimal
Dominated By The Obscene

This Is The Mind Of A Spiritual Animal
Anotha' Hybrid, Anotha' Species. ☆

HOPE

I Guess Its' Kinda Rough

To Know This Life Is So Tough

They Seem To Torture Us

Jus' For Fallin' In Love

They Could Be Callin' Ya' Bluff

To Make It Harda' For Us

I Guess U've Had Enough

If You Can't Get What You Want

U're Askin' Me Who Can You Trust

When All Aroun' Its' So Dangerous

Well Surely As U're Breath

Will Turn To Dust

This Is The World

That Doesn't Need Us

I Know Its' Kinda Hard To Belong

When Everyone Aroun' You

Is Treatin' You Wrong

I Know Its' Kinda Hard To Hold On

When You Bein' Kept Down For So Long

They're Killin Us As We're Livin'

They're Savin' Us As We're Dyin'

They're Grantin' Our Freedoms

An' Takin' Control

They're Leavin' Us In Limbo

They Promise Us Nothin'

They're Helpin' Us To Believe

Without A Hope. ☆

SNAKES AN' LADDERS

♣♠♣

You Know Its' A Privilege To Be Here
In Spite Of The Places Where I've Bein'
You Know Its' Really Nice To See You Again
Despite All The Things I've Already Seen

When U're Standing At A Crossroads
There's Only One Way You Can Go
You Can Always Go Straight Ahead
Or Take Some Other Path
U've Never Taken Before

You Know I Really Hate To Say It
But I Guess I'm Gonna Say It Anyway
You Know I Really Didn't Mean It
But It Just Turned Out To Be That Way

An' All The Colours Of U're Rainbow
Every Shade An' Every Hue
All The Colours Of U're Rainbow
Has Left Me Confused
Which Colour I Should Choose

You Know I'm More Than Grateful
For All Of The Small Things
An' All The Tall Things Too
You Know I'm More Than Thankful
For A Chance To Meet, Somebody Like You

Even Though Its' Hard To Say
From All Those Times When I Walked Away
Well I Guess I Really Should Have Stayed All Along
The Stakes Are High, So Take Me Higher
The Stakes Are High, So We Keep On Climbing

We Always Fall Down Jus' Like Snakes An' Ladders
We Always Fall Down But We Always Get Up Again
Jus' Like Snakes An' Ladders We Always Fall Down
But We Always Get Up Again. ☆

U'RE ASSOCIATIONS

Anotha' Random Accident

Anotha' Local Incident

Did Anybody Here

Witness A Crime

It Could Be Mass Illusion

It Could Be Mass Confusion

To Look The Otha' Way

With A Blind Eye

For Those Who Never Wait

To Get The Story Straight

Always Seem To Make Up

Their Own Inventions

It Could Be Catastrophic

It Could Be Hyperbolic

But The Cop's On Show Up

As A Deterrent

As Long As These Fools

Wanna Silence The Truth

The Gossips Goin' Aroun'

Jus' Like Chinese Whispers

It Could Be Somethin' Ironic

It Could Be Catatonic

But Nobody Here

Wants To Speak Up Now

So You Wonda'

What's Bein' Goin' Down

By The Definition Of

U're Speculations

But Nobody Here

Wants To Get Involved

By The Reasons Of

U're Associations. ☆

CHEMICAL ROMANCE

Its' Jus' Anotha Wack Scene
On Anotha' Flat Screen

Somethin' To Wind You Up
In Someone Else's Dream

I Wanna Go To The City
I Wanna Ride In U're Car

I Wanna Hang In The Club
An' Take A Seat At The Bar

Its' Jus' A Digital Nation
Of Wise Crackin' Quotations

The Latest P.C Game
That You Can't Stop Playin'

I Wanna Go To The Beach
I Wanna Hang In The Park

I Wanna Swim In The Sea
Chillin' Under The Stars

I Couldn't Love You Any Less
Than I Loved You Before

An' If I Love You Right Now Baby
I Couldn't Love You Anymore

I Wanna Tick When You Tock
Pick You Up When U're Down

An' If Its' Cool To Be A Fool Baby
Let's Keep Foolin' Aroun'

Where The Sound Of The Beat
Puts You In A Trance

An' The Music Is Played
An' We Begin A Dance

So We Can Synergize
A Chemical Romance

So Let's Take A Chance
An' Try To Make It Last. ☆

DUST AN' STONE

♣♠♣

I Throw The Stones Into The Sea

An' The Birds All Flock Violently

As These Passers By Look An' Wonda' Why

Is Eternity On The Otha' Side

What Seems To Be Is Out Of Reach

But The Sea Has Washed Up On The Beach

Its' Now The Calm Before The Storm

As I Watch Her Waitin' From Dusk Til' Dawn

A Minute Of Silence For Us To Mourn

The End Of Time An' The Seconds Born

As Much As Time Is Cruel An' Kind

The Stones Remind Me Of Somethin' Divine

I've Walked With Friends

An' I've Walked Alone

Still This World Is Hard To Know

Coz Everythin' That I Use To Own

Has Surely Turned To Dust An' Stone. ☆

GOOD CHARACTER

♣♠♣

Well I Guess Its' Anotha' Hung Jury
Somewhere In The Courts Of Public Opinion

An' What Could Be Bought Or Sold
Anotha' Case Closed For A Couple Of Million

I Guess We Can All Be Accused
By The Definition Of Our Associations

I Guess When The Shit Hits The Fan
That's When They Start Closin' Down All The Curtains

Standin' In The Light Of Smokin' Gun
An' Now There's An' Elephant Inside Of The Room

Well I Guess There's No Smoke Without Any Fire
For All Of The Liars Who Covet The Truth

Will The Last One Out Turn Off The Lights
Now They're Throwin' Shade Upon U're Good Character

Still My Alibi Is Lookin' Kinda' Tight
Still I Might Be In Need Of A Good Barrister. ☆

LOSIN' YOU
♣♠♣

I Thought I Could Call You

I Thought That We

Should Talk It Through

I Guess By Now

You Know Me

In U're Own Way

Bein' Feelin'

Lost An' Lonely

Jus' Doin' My Own Thing

But Then I Realized

I Ain't Got Much To Say

So What Mo' Can I Say

Well I Guess

Its' Kinda' Strange

Now That I've Become

So Predictable

I Guess I'm

Jus' Like The Others

Compared To All

Of U're Lovers

I Guess Everybody Needs

Somebody New

Once Upon A Time

You Know I Might

Have Paid The Price

For Saving The Life

Or The Likes Of You

Now Suicide

Might Be Heavy

But You Know Its' Kinda' Friendly

When Sumthin' So Deadly

Crawls Into U're Mind

Jus' The Other Day

I Began To Pray

Down On My Knees

But I Prayed In Vain

I Guess I Needed The Time

To Figure Out What's Right

I Guess My Only Problem

Was Facin' The Truth

Cos I Bein' Livin' This Dream

Jus' To Figure Out

What It Means

Faraway From A Life

That I Once Knew

An' I Bein' Chasin' The Scene

Of Those Who Dare To Dream

But All Of The While

I Bein' Losin' You. ☆

AGAIN

♧♤♧

I Love You Mo', I Loved You Before
So Much Mo', Than I Could Stand

I Love This Game, We Always Play
You Always Seem To Take My Heart Away

How Do We Surpass The Past
An' How Do We Embrace This Future

Even Though We Know It Ain't Fair
So Why Should We Care What Anybody's Thinking

As Real As It Seems, Its' Not Just A Dream
But It Feels Like It Is, Til I Wake Up Again

Facing The Day, Walking Away
To Follow The Path That You Made

Somehow We Know It Always Ends In Tears
So Dry U're Eyes An' Forget U're Fears

Somehow We Know, We Were Never Prepared
To See It Through, All Over Again. ☆

ITS' NOT CONVENIENT

♣♠♣

Drawin' Closer To

The Evenin' Of My Life

Still Tryin' To Survive

An' Its' Half Past Five

For All The Things I Said

Full Of Compliments

But You Don't Want My Love

Its' Not Convenient

Anotha' Day Arrives

An' Its' Already Night

Its' Not So Much Of A Struggle

But Mo' Of A Fight

I Guess Its' Crystal Clear

That You Could Never Commit

No You Don't Want My Love

Its' Not Convenient

Now There's Only One Question

That Springs To Mind

Did I Get It Wrong

Or Did I Get It Right

Now It Seems That Sorrow

Will Follow Me Down

Tomorrow Comes Aroun'

Still I'm Tryin' To Figure It Out

Thinkin' Bout' The Years

That I Left Behind

Doin' Overtime

Regrets On My Mind

For All The Things You Said

Doesn't Make Any Sense

You Don't Want My Love

Its' Not Convenient. ☆

ROMANTIC STAR
(FILTHY MOUTH)

You Got U're Grubby Hands All Over It
You Got U're Sticky Fingers All Stuck In It
You Can't But Help, Muddle It Aroun'
Without Makin' A Sound, From U're Filthy Mouth

You Played U're Dirty Tricks In The Thick Of It
The Low Down Dirty Shame You Was Up To It
You Can't But Help To Keep On Foolin' Aroun'
Without Makin' A Sound, From U're Filthy Mouth

If Anyone Is To Blame There's A Name For It
The Lie An' Cheatin' Game, There's A Face That Fits'
An' Its' No Wonda' You Keep Messin' Aroun'
Without Makin' A Sound, From U're Filthy Mouth

An' All You Lovers, You Know Who You Are
U've Come So Near But U're Still So Far
An' All You Lovers, You Know Who You Are
An' You Know U've Bein' Banished
From That Romantic Star. ☆

BORN TO FADE

♧♤♧

In My Younger Days

When I Was Someone Else

Now I'm An' Avatar

Of My Former Self

Sadistic Masochistic

So Unaware

As They Hold Me Hostage

To The Bondage Of Despair

Calmly An' Quietly

As I Take That Walk

Pass The Bloodthirsty Vampires

By My Door

Using Me As Their Bait

To Get What They Want

As My Ghostly Companions

Await Their Reward

From The Castin' Down

Of A Beautiful Angel

With The 3rd Of A Stock

From A Fallen Stable

Since You Were Destined

To Fly Like A Dragon In The Sky

Like The Story Of Icarus

I Mus' Have Flown To High

I Guess I Am What I Am

In U're Master Plan

An' Even If I Change

I Remain The Same

An' Emotional Thing

A Visceral Human Being

Jus' As You Numbered My Days

Well I Was Born To Fade. ☆

THE FALL
♣♤♣

I Guess Nobody Made You Care
About The Things That You Do

I Guess You Couldn't Care A Less
Well I Guess That's Nuthin' New

I Guess What Always Goes Around
Is Somehow Coming Into View

I Guess That's Why There's
So Much Distance Between Me An' You

You Can Always Raise U're Voice
You Can Always Vent U're Anger

You Can Always Put Me Down
Dragging Me Around, Through That Quagmire

Even When You Try To Offload
An' Put All The Weight On Me

You Could Always Switch It Up A Gear Or Two
Until There's Nuthin' Left In-Between

You Know It Doesn't Matter Who Said It First
As Long As Its' All Bein' Understood

We Could Both Be Right Or Wrong
If The Circumstances Could Balance The Books

I Guess You Didn't Bet
That Safety Net Was There At All

I Guess You Didn't Think
That I Would Catch You, Even After The Fall. ☆

SENSE OF HUMOUR

♣♧♣

I Know U're Second Guessin'

Some Of My Suggestions

Jus' As You Like To Question

My Point Of View

I Guess I Could Be

Anotha' Serial Realist

Or Somethin' Mo'

U're Jus' Not Use Too

I Guess Nobody Believed

That They Could Be Deceived

But In The Name Of Love

Isn't Everybody Guilty

But Its' Never Too Late

To Set The Record Straight

But How Long Will You Wait

To Find A Perfect Mate

Why Do We All Do The Same Things

All Over Again

Thinkin' It Might Turn Out Different

Somehow In The End

I Guess This Wishful Thinkin'

Is Jus' A Human Condition

Or Somethin' That We're Missin'

Instinctively

I Wasn't Laughin' At You

But The Things That You Do

Even Though Its' Not Funny

Its' Ironically True

I Guess My Sense Of Humour

Comes With A Lot Of Stupor

I Guess The Jokes On Me

But Its' Lost On You. ☆

A REASON TO CRY

♧♤♧

The Song Sang The Blues
The Song Every Shade An' Hue
The Song Was Always True
It Was All About Me An' You

The Song I Always Knew
The Song Would See Us Through
The Song Like Some Kind Of Voodoo
The Song Took Hold, Like The Sweetest Taboo

The Song Set The Scene
The Song Was Like A Dream
The Song Vulgar An' Obscene
The Song Sailed Away, An' Endless Melody

Here Comes The Clean Up Man
With His Hammer An' Sickle
He Ain't No Middle Man
This Ain't No Slap An' Tickle

Here Comes The Mastermind
Of U're One True Crime
But The Devil Doesn't Have
A Reason To Cry. ☆

IT DOESN'T MATTER

♣♠♣

It Doesn't Matter

If Anyone Knows

Cos We've All Bein' There

Once Before

It Doesn't Matter

What Anyone Believes

It Doesn't Matter

Cos We've All Bein' Deceived

It Doesn't Matter

If Anyone Cares

We're Already Livin'

With The Same Ole' Fears

An' It Doesn't Matter

Where You Belong

It Doesn't Matter

Who's Right

An' Who's Wrong

It Doesn't Matter

Whatever You Say

If Nobody's

Listenin' Anyway

It Doesn't Matter

Whatever You Do

Its' Only The Truth

That's Remindin' You

A By-Product Of Love

Turns To Hate

An' Rejections Finds You

Waitin' At The Gate

How The Mighty An' High

Have Bein'

Brought Down So Low

But It Doesn't Matter

There's No Place To Go

No It Doesn't Matter

We're All On Our Own. ☆

WINNIN' TEAM

♧♤♧

Despite The Time When 6 Was 9
God Was Satisfied With U're No.7
Besides The Vulgar An' Divine
The Thorn In U're Side
From Roses Made In Heaven

For Those Of Us
With A Terminal Condition
A Suicidal Mission
Only Goes To Show
U're Only Innit'
For The Capital Decapitations
While Every Homeless Person
Is Still Without A Hope

In The Kangaroo Court
Of Public Cynicism
Cryin' Crocodile Tears
From All The Onion Peel
It Seems That We
Have Underestimated
The Fortunes Of Our Success
Is From The Money We Steal

Whatever The Nexus
Of The Latest Generation
Anotha' War Of The Sexes
Is Jus' A Primal Scream
A Pre-Selection
For U're Circumcision
Before They Lock Up U're Freedoms
An' Throw Away The Key

But Were You Silenced By
The Latest Gaggin' Orders
Did They Try To Bribe You
With Some Cheap Gasoline
Or Did You Try To Place
Anotha' Bet On The Side
To Guarantee You Was Down
With The Winnin' Team. ☆

HEATHENS

♧♤♧

When Was It Ever Really Fair

When Did Anyone Ever Really Care

When Did Anyone Ever Dare

To Rise Above It All

Or Make That Call

When Were They Gonna

Wipe Away U're Tears

When Were They Gonna

Address U're Greatest Fears

As They're Buildin' Their Dreams

On The Backs Of The Broken

Towers An' Walls

But The Gates Never Open

Could It Be That The Needy

Are In Debt To The Greedy

Committin' No Crime

Except For Being Poor

Its' A Wonda' Who They're Hurtin'

Preachin' To The Converted

Removin' What Was Certain

What We Depended On

How Did These

Heathens Of Heaven

Ever Make Their Gains

To Put Us In Bondage

Into Mental Chains

Who Will These

Heathens Of Heaven

Summons Today

Or Simply Make Their Sanctions

If We Don't Pay. ☆

UNCONSCIOUS BIAS

From The Depths Of Despair
An' The Restless Unease
Arousing U're Anger
An' Disturbing The Peace

Aggravating U're Nature
An' Igniting U're Temper
Enflamin' The Anxieties
Inside Of U're Soul

A Vexatious Spirit
Now Brings You Discomfort
A Voice Of Aggression
Is U're Countenance Perturbed

As U're Personality
Is Now Out Of Character
From A Basic Instinct
An' A Primal Scream

From The Institutionalised
Unconscious Bias
Systemic Profiling
Of The World We Live In. ☆

ANGELS AN' DEMONS
♣♤♣

Baby I'm Not Pretendin'

That This World Isn't Endin'

But Is It Worth Defendin'

Down To The Last Drop

Baby I'm Not Recedin'

Believin' No Ones Receivin'

This Message That I Got

From Planet Earth

I'm Not Makin' Decisions

Of Politics An' Religions

I'm Jus' Hopin' This Message

Will Penetrate U're Heart

I Know The Birth Rates Declinin'

But Have You Made Up U're Mind Yet

Is It Still Worthwhile

To Have Mines An' U'res

I Don't Need You To Save Me

Not Now Or Maybe Lately

I'm Jus' Closin' The Windows

An' Lockin' The Doors

Waitin' So Patiently

There's Love An' Hate In Me

Tryin' To Come To Terms

With My God

I'm Not Defeated By

Angels An' Demons

I'm Only Gettin' Sick

Coz I Jus' Caught A Cold

I'm Not Frightened By

The Storms An' The Lightnin'

I'm Jus' Watchin' The Time

As We're Growin' Old. ☆

WITHOUT A CARE
♣♠♣

Somewhere Ahead Of Time
Left Behind In The Middle Of Nowhere
Walkin' In A One Way Direction
I Had To Tear Myself Apart
Jus' To Turn Me Aroun'

I Was Crucified, Buried Alive
Inside Of My Mind
I Was Accused An' Abused
Superficially Wounded
For Droppin' My Guard

Sometimes It Eats You Alive
Jus' Like Cancer Inside Of U're Bones
Surprised By Anotha' Disguise
Now That You Find
This World Wasn't Made For You

You Can Sleep With Somebody
Until You End Up Sleepin' Alone
You Can Call Up Anybody
Until You Don't Wanna Answer The Phone

You Can Take It, Or Leave It
You Can Wish That You Never Got Involved
You Can Keep Kickin' That Ball
Without A Care In The World. ☆

CITY OF SIN

♣♤♣

I Guess He's Jus' A Dreamer

An' Yes He's Probably Seen Her

In The Blink Of An Eye

She Passes Him By

Alone An' So Remote

In A Place Of His Own

I Guess No Man Is An' Island

But He's A Sole Survivor

U've Bein' Here Before

An' U've Unlock The Door

Unsurprised By Things

That You Want To Explore

For Now Once You Were Blind

But Now She's Opened U're Eyes

Revealin' The Secrets

You Were Hopin' To Find

The Scarlet An' The Fever

Makes You Think That You Need Her

An' Somethin' In Her Eyes

Makes You Wanna Stay

Its' Called The Art Of Seduction

As She Makes Her Introduction

But Nobody Mentions

The Beauty Of Decay

An' The Journey Of A Thousand Miles

Begins With One Step

As Much As He Knows

Fortune Favours The Brave

As Much As Who Dares

Is Hopin' To Win

Welcome To The City Of

The City Of Sin. ☆

DUE DILLIGENCE

♣♠♣

They Say The Watchman Comes
With The Forces An' The Nature Of Love
They Say The Seeds We Sow
Have Already Taken Their Toll
The Merest Thought
Of The Hangman's Rope
At The End Of The Road
We Thought We Couldn't Cope
For All Hope We Could Not See
The Thought Of Watchman
Watching Over Me
From The Anger
That Turns Into Violence
From The Roses Growing
Surrounded By Violets
From The Fountain Of Youth
The Watchman Told
Eternity Was Only Growing Old
With All Due Diligence
Were Turning The Pages
The One That Takes Us
Across All The Ages
From All The Issues That Governs
The Heart He Often Imparts. ☆

THE BLUES
(SIMPLIFICATIONS)
♣♠♣

I Bein' Knockin' U're Door

I Bein' Callin' U're Phone

Wonderin' When U'll Be Back Home

I Guess I'm All Out Of Seasons

An' I Got Nuthin' To Do

But Love Is The Reasons

Why I Got The Blues

I Was Down In The Dumps

I Was The King Of The Heap

For Mo' Than 24 Hours

I Bein' Losin' Sleep

I'm Goin' Out Of My Head

I'm Feelin' Like A Fool

But Love Is The Reasons

Why I Got The Blues

I Guess I'm Goin' Nowhere

The Lights Are Changin' Now

Its' Jus' A City Of Strangers

An' I'm Lost In This Town

Its' Jus' An' Empty Glass

My Recollections Of You

But Love Is The Reasons

Why I Got The Blues

Its' Jus' The Thought Of You

That Makes Me Wanna Submit

U're Such A Beautiful Thing

An' I Don't Wanna Quit

I'm Lettin' Down My Guard

But I Don't Wanna Trip

Its' Jus' The Simplifications

Of An' Ordinary Thing. ☆

THE WICKED OR THE GOOD
♧♤♧

It Doesn't Belong To You
It Doesn't Belong To Me

You Might Try To Put A Price On It
But I Tell You Now, It Jus' Happens To Be

I Guess U're Born Into It
I Guess It All Comes Naturally

No Matter How You Try To Shape It
We Jus' Inherit, A Small Or Bigger Piece

No Matter How We Try To Change It
It Always Seems To Remain The Same

No Matter How Much We Make A Mark
It Always Seems Too Hardly Make A Stain

Of All The Blood We Would Spill
It Just Seems Like, We've Lost The Will

If The Fires Desire Is Just To Kill
Destroying Everything We've Ever Made

Now There's No One Left To Accuse
Because Of The Things That We Do
As We Learn To Live A Disappointed Lie
Abusing The Truth, We've Always Denied

Even Within The Darkest Hours
We Always Bow Down To Unnatural Powers

As We Learn To Submit The Freedoms We Gained
By Simply Giving Our Sovereigns Away

I Guess Its' Hard To Really Know
Whatever Commands U're Living Soul

It Could Be The Wicked Or The Good
I Guess We'll Never Really Know. ☆

THE FULLNESS

♣♠♣

Not To Confuse With Confusion

Not To Delude Castin' Illusions

Not To Deceive Or Set Aside

Cos There's No Place For Me Left To Hide

Well Its' A One Way Miracle

This Unconditional Thing Called Love

An' I Believe Its' That Its' Masterful

That's Why It Seems Were One Of A Kind

An' Should I Fail To Prevail

Will This Fairytale Come Tumblin' Down

If None Would Seek To Take Pity On Me

If Such A Lowly Servant Serves No Purpose Now

I'm Lovin' You With The Fullness

With All The Fullness Of My Time

Lovin' You Mo' Than The Fullness

An' The Fullness Thereof Of My Life. ☆

WHEN ITS' GONE

♧♤♧

We're Not Strangers To Love
We're Not Lovers Of Pain

We're Not Use To This Loneliness
But We Always End Up This Way

We Don't Care About Tomorrow
We're Only Thinking Of Today

We're Not Holding Onto Forever
But We Always Wish It Would Never Fade

There's No Reasons For This Madness
There's No Reasons To Be Sad

There's No Reasons, Why We Can't Fix This
An' Put Those Broken Pieces Together Again

No One Said, It Was Gonna Be Easy
We Always Want, What We Can't Have

An' Were Not Fools To This Heartache
Its' Only Love, When Its' Gone. ☆

MYSELF
♣♠♣

I Know That You Want

What's Best For Me

Before I Fallen To My Knees

The Freedom To Choose

What's Hard To Believe

Between God An' Man

The Devil An' The Deep Blue Sea

What's Offendin' You

Might Be Pleasin' Me

Sometimes Its' Hard To Know

The Difference In-Between

Its' Kinda' Hard To Give It Up

An' Stop Lettin' You Down

Its' Jus' Anotha' Crossroads

An' I'm A Sinner Now

I'm Blowin' Hot An' Cold

Before You Spittin' Me Out

I Know My Days Are Numbered

An' U're Countin' Me Down

Like A Fish Out Of Water I'm In Misery

Like Those Stars In The Sky

A Sea Of Galilee

Now I'm Thinkin' Its' Strange

That You Want Me To Change

To Be A Little Bit Better

Than I Was Before

What Can I Do Or Say

If You Made Me That Way

Thought I Was Doin' Okay

Tryin' To Be Myself. ☆

WISEMAN

♧♤♧

The Sum Of My Life In 5 Mins
The Saddest Story Ever Told
The Silent Anger Quietly Rages
In A Moment Of Madness
I Turn To No One I Know
Having Disappeared Into Obscurity
No One Knows U're Name
Or Place Of Abode
A Dead Walking Into Darkness
In A Moment Of Weakness
I Turn To No One I Know
Behind These Walls
Where U've Lock Me In
Behind These Walls
Where You Tear Me Down
While U're Trying To Break
My Back An' My Spirit
In A Moment Of Temptation
I Turn To No One I Know
U're Knowledge Increases
An' It Fills You With Sorrow
To Carry The Burdens Of Tomorrow
For The Wiseman Who Said
An' Old Head On Young Shoulders
Is Too Much Weight To Carry Alone. ☆

KARMA AN' FATE
(U'RE BEST LIE)
♣♠♣

From The Moment The Apple

Fell From The Tree

From The Moment U're Ego

Turned Into Vanity

Exchanin' U're Soul

For Diamonds An' Pearls

Divorcin' U're God

To Marry The World

As The Age Of Consent

Is Marked Upon U're Grave

For All Those Undyin' Flames

True Love Remains

As All These I Love You's

Becomes A Paradox

Sacrificin' The One

To Get What You Want

From The Comforts Of

A Place Of U're Own

As 8 Billion People

Are Sleepin' Alone

Now That U're Bendin' The Rules

That Was Already Broken

Still Ignorin' The Truth

That Was Already Spoken

As Karma An' Fate

Wait By U're Door

Boycottin' The Deals

That You Made Before

Now I See That U're Livin'

U're Best Lie

The One That You Couldn't

Afford To Buy. ☆

SINCERITY

Why Do Bad Things Happen To Good People
To Turn Their Hearts An' Faith Away
Could It Be The Laws Of Human Nature
Or Some Random Events That's Pre-Ordained
Its' A Wonder Why U're Sincerity
Is Such An' Honest Innocent Thing
Or Why U're Kindness Is Taken For Weakness
Is It Jus' To Keep U're Anger At Bay
Why Do Good Things Happen To Bad People
An' Do You Believe They Can Ever Change
Or Could It Be The Laws Of Karma
Resigning Us To Our Fate
Its' A Wonder Why U're Sincerity
Is Such An' Honest Innocent Thing
Or Why U're Kindness Is Taken For Weakness
Jus' To Keep U're Frustrations Away
Could This Be A Chaos Theory
That No One Here Can Understand
An' Why Is This World So Topsy-Turvy
If The Law Of Averages Doesn't Makes Any Sense
Its' A Wonder Why U're Sincerity
Is Such An' Honest Innocent Thing
Or Why U're Kindness Is Taken For Weakness
Is It Jus' To Please Us Or Treat Us All The Same. ☆

THE THOUGHT POLICE

♣♠♣

As This Future World

Prepares Its' Laws

Like Some Orwellian Fiction

Born In 84'

As The Man Machine

Who Dreams Of Brazil

Knows The Only Thing We Die For

Is The Freedom Of Will

Somewhere Down In A Cell

Where You Were Being Held

While Some Anonymous Donor

Paid U're Bail

Seems You Were Bought An' Sold

In A Private Sale

Like Some Commodity

From The Handmaids Tale

An' Now This Science Fiction

Of Their Objectives

A Singularity

To Meet Their Directives

Or Jus' Anotha' Precursor

For A Future Crime

A Minority Report

Designed To Change Our Minds

As U're Desensitised

From All That You See

With All The Censors Inside

To Tell You What's Real

As You Fall For The Stars

On U're T.V Screen

Beneath The Watchful Eyes

Of The Thought Police. ☆

THE DEVIL LIVED
♣♠♣

Of All Signs In The Sky
Could This Be The Wrath Of Love
The Weaving Of A Prophecy
Or The Infancy Of A Fairytale
There Me Be A Resurrection
After All We Could Forgive
A Thousand Years We've Left Behind
An' The Reasons Why The Devil Lived

Its' The Oldest Relics That Are Left Behind
Discovered By A Lost Generation
Its' Something For The Sceptics To Deny
Something Set Aside, For You To Believe In
An' There Me Be A Restoration
As The Water Flows Underneath The Bridge
Like Those Passages In The Sands Of Time
For The Days An' The Ages When The Devil Lived

Tomorrows Future Is Yesterdays Pass
Rising Up From Defeat Out Of The Ashes
An' The Eruptions Of The Peace Of Wars
The Beginning Of A Happy Ending
An' There Me Be Some Form Of Agreement
A Brokered Seal For A Covenant
Some Kind Of Deal For Humankind
The Reasons Why The Devil Lived. ☆

INNOCENT

It Seems They Want

To Coerce An' Control

The Spirit Residin'

Inside Of U're Soul

Maintainin' Their

Powers Over You

Until You Fall Into

Their Power Struggle

They Try To Influence

All The Things That You Do

But Why Should You Frett

If U've Got Nothin' To Lose

In U're Doubts An' Regrets

You Mus' Learn To Rebuke

All Of The Obstacles

That You Have To Remove

Now They're Conjurin' Up

A Web Of Lies

For The Weakest Ones

With The Meekest Minds

Jus' To Trip You Up

Into A Suicide

The Cause Of All Deception

A Caution To The Wise

As They're Holding You Now

In Their Contempt

Of Emotional Blackmail

Wid' A Guilty Conscience

But Can't You See Their Time

Is Already Spent

Explotin' The Minds

Of All The Innocent. ☆

NO GOOD REASON

I Guess It Ain't What You Can Do For God
But Mo' About What God Can Do For You

I've Paid My Debts To Society
But Society Has Never Paid Its' Debts To Me

Now Mo' Or Less I've Tasted The Best
An' I Can Tell You Its' So Bitter Sweet

With The Alcohol Upon My Lips
An' The Fact She Belonged To Another Jockey

When You Catch A Glimpse Of A Beautiful Thing
An' The Guilty Thoughts You Keep Having

When You Want It All But Its' Too Far To Fall
That's The Moral Of The Whole Damn Story

I Have To Confess, This Love Is A Mess
An' All What's Left Is Jus' Broken Pieces

What's Lived An' Died, A Thousand Times
We All Repeat, For No Good Reason. ☆

NUMBER ONE
♣♤♣

Like Holy Fire

Rainin' Down From The Sky

Everythin' Gonna Burn

Everythins' Gonna Drown

So When You Threatin' To Leave

Its' Kinda Hard To Believe

That You Can't Find The Keys

To The Front

U're Always Tellin' Me

I'm Only Half A Man

An' Nuthin' Like The King

That I Was Before

An' Like A Government Plan

Now The Monies All Spent

Like The Dreams We Had

Now We Don't Have A Hope

Should Anybody Care

About U're Marital Affairs

When They're All Having

Affairs Of Their Own

Like Those Serial Killers

On U're Prime Time T.V

Its' Jus' A Soap Box Opera

To Keep An' Audience At Home

But After The Storm Is Surely Done

Its' No Wonder You Go

Before U've Surely Come

An' After U've Done A Million Sums

Its' No Wonder You Can't Count

From Zero To Number One. ☆

SUBSTITUTION

♣♠♣

In My Despair I'm Truly Aware
Misery Is Looking For Company

One Thousand Miles Of Forgotten Smiles
Now That My Love Is A Distant Memory

I Thought I Was Free Until I Couldn't See
High Above The Clouds Surrounding An' Drowning Me

But I Hope It Will Pass, I Hope It Don't Last
All This Loneliness Living Inside Of Me

How Can It Be All The Things That I See
Have Isolated Me While I'm Taking This Journey

Now Its' Hard To Escape The Shape Of My Fate
I'm Facing My Mistakes Contemplating My Destiny

So Whatever It Takes Don't Ever Give It Up
For The Past Is Behind An' The Futures In Front

An' Whatever It Takes, Jus' Give It All You Got
With Nothing To Compare, No Substitution For Love. ☆

THE CRADLE

Eternity You Will Find

Flowin' Through U're Mind

Like The River Nile

If Only For A Time Times

An' Half A Time

You Was Once A Man

Twice A Child

On That Seventh Day

You Were 7 Years Old

You Was Only A Child

When The Story Was Told

Runnin' Wild An' Runnin' Free

Like That River Nile

To Eternity

Come That Day

When You Would Realize

The Age Of 33

Would Open U're Eyes

When All That We Love

We Would Sacrifice

For Eternity

For The River Nile

Born In The Cradle

Of The Womb

Is Where U're Spirit

Was Entombed

Until The Day

That You Should Wake

From The Cradle

Of The Grave. ☆

REINVENTION

U're A Victim Of Circumstance
An' The Circumstances Has Made You A Victim

Were All Jus' Creatures Here Of Appetite
Addicted To Each Others Personalities

Even Though U're Aware There's None To Compare
Is That A Hint Of Contempt In U're Vocabulary

With The Best Of Intentions They Always Mention
U're The Object Of Their Every Fantasy

With Style An' Grace You Command The Space
As' U're Somewhat Poised So Elegantly

With Every Word That's Seldom Heard
Their Always Hanging On So Desperately

Seems U've Become The Centre Of Attention
U're The Life An' The Soul, The Whole Party

Somehow The Controversy Of U're Habitual Habits
Is Jus' A Reinvention Of Who You Use To Be. ☆

CONCRETE

♣♠♣

A River Meanders

Weaving Into Streams

Mother Nature Is Strangled

An' Polluted At The Seams

A Displaced Union

Of What Use To Be

A Kingdom Rising

Out Of The Sea

The Poverty Of A Ghetto

Is Filled With Urban Myths

An' All Riddled With Litter

For The Back Streets Kids

Amongst The Debris An' Fragments

Were Left To Commune

Besides The Rush Hour Traffic

We're All Consumed

Graffiti Taggs'

Become Museum Pieces

Printed An' Posted

All Over The Wall

Neon Signs

A Dystopic Future

Where Paradise

Has Come An' Gone

An' The City Towers

Are Like Giants In The Sky

Choking The Air

An' Blocking The Light

Beneath The Echelons

Of A High Society

The Golden Roads

Are Trampled Into Concrete. ☆

NUTHIN' TO SHOW

♧♤♧

I Just Got Out The County Jail
Cos A Friend Of Mine, Jus' Paid The Bail
An' All Of These Things I Was Grateful For
Now I'm No Longer Runnin'
From The Hands Of The Law

Well This Mus' Be A Bran' New Start
Since Me An' My Girl, Well We Had To Part
It Musta' Broke Her Heart When They Put Me Away
But Now That I'm Back, I'm Here To Stay

I Got Me A Job, 1 Day A Week
For The Other 6 Days, I'm Jus' Losin' Sleep
I Got Me A Room On The 2nd Floor
But I'm Payin' Dues While I'm Keepin' Score

It Could Be My Last Or My Second Chance
It Could Be My Future Instead Of My Past
Still I'm Barely Survivin' With Enough To Get By
But I'm Jus' Happy To Be Livin' My Life

I Guess Its' Time For Me To Change
Since I Read That Book From Ole' King James
They Say You Always Reap What You Sow
But I Got Nuthin', Nuthin' To Show. ☆

I KNOW

Love Is Gone

An' I Don't Know How Long

Its' Gonna Take Me

To Get Back Home

Whatever The Meaning

I Jus' Lost The Feelin'

Of What I Was Dreamin' All Along

Love Has Forsaken

If I'm Not Mistaken

I Felt My Soul Breakin'

My Spirit Inside

I Thought That I Made It

The Way That I Played It

Until You Laid

The Blame At My Door

Love Has Departed

An' Left Me Broken Hearted

I Guess Its' Down To Me

An' Myself Alone

I Thought I Could Handle It

I Thought I Could Stand Up

But Instead, Its' Keepin' Me Down

I Turned From The Darkness

Into The Light

An' Now I'm Walkin' Down

The Highways Of Life

But Its' Too Far To Reach It

An' Its' Leavin' Me Speechless

Its' Hard To Resist

The Love I Know. ☆

OUT TO LUNCH

♣♠♣

How Could You Have Too Many
If You Never Had Any
When There Seems To Be
Plenty Goin' Aroun'
We Tried So Hard To Untangle
From The Last Jingle Jangle
We Trip The Light Fandango
For A Night On The Town

I've Only Set Aside
What You Thought You Were Denied
I Thought You Might Decide
To Do It Again
The River Of Emotions
Of Deep Erotic Devotion
Somehow That Sun Tan Lotion
Made Everythin' Bronze

I Musta' Tripped An' Fell
Into A Fairytale
It Cost Me 200 Bucks
Jus' To Get Out Of Jail
An' By The Skin Of My Teeth
This Fantasy Wasn't Cheap

Now That I Lost My Ideals
An' Found My Belief
That's When She Hit Me Up
Its' When I Tried My Luck
Before The Breakfast Was Made
She Took Me Out To Lunch
After The Rubaduck'
In The Jacuzzi Tub
Suckin' On That Lollipop
An' Potions Of Love. ☆

FOR THE BEST
♧♤♧

The Trust Is Broken
   From Harsh Words Spoken

      A Letter With A Note In
         A Pitiful Explanation

No Four Leaf Clover
   The Honeymoon Is Over

      The Wind Is Much Colder
         On A Lonesome Road

The Memories You Found In
   Are Sinkin' An' Drownin'

      Remindin' You How An' When
         Now An' Then Use To Be

You Feel Like U're Fadin'
   Maybe U're Heart Is Breakin'

      The Mistakes We Both Made
         Was Already In Repeat

Its' Hard To Believe In
   When U're Losin' The Feelin'

      When You Know Love Is Fleetin'
         From U're Heart

Tryin' Hard To Be Free
    Still Hopin' No One Can See

        The Pain An' Misery
           That's Draggin' You Down

But Don't You Give Up Now
    Its' Time To Look Up Now

        As The Tears Slowly Roll Down
           Like The Rain On U're Face

I Know U're Runnin' On Empty
    Its' Not The Way It Was Meant To Be

        But It Might Jus' Be
        For The Best.☆

ME

♣♤♣

I'm Takin' One Step
One Day At A Time
As Pourin' U're Knowledge
Into My Mind
Redefinin' The Merits
For All The Good
That I've Done
Still My Heart Is Contrite
Was I Right Or Wrong

Between The Gates
Of Heaven An' Hell
I'm Pourin' The Waters
Into The Well
Even Though You Said
You Would Never Forsake
Was It My Mistakes
Believin' What You Forgave

It Was Only In Silence
I Was Tryin' To Heed
As You Was Pourin' U're Heart
Into My Dreams
Still I Got Some Regrets
About Somethin' You Said
Knowin' The Road Up Ahead
Only Fills Me With Dread

An' What About Me
An' All The Things That I Need
All The Things I Need
Jus' To Be Happy
An' What About Me
An' All The Things That I See
Has Fallen Apart All Aroun' Me.☆

PREVAIL

♧♤♧

I Remembered A Song

Singin' This Life Is Long

Remindin' Me

Death Cannot Be Cheated

From The Day That U're Born

The Words Were Already Sung

So Could It Be

We're Already Defeated

I Believe That Time

Has No Reason Or Rhyme

Although U're One Of Kind

In This Universe

But Whatever We Face

Within This Human Race

Time Could Always Replace

In The Blink Of An' Eye

The Philosophy's

We Were Taught To Believe

In Ideologies

From Beyond The Veil

A Spiritual Need

Of Inherited Things

To Set Us Apart

From This Material World

Well Take A Seat

An' Listen Well

For This Is U're Story

An' Not A Fairytale

An' Listen Close

Coz It Might Serve You Well

For Us To Survive

For Us To Prevail.☆

I LOVE YOU

I Never Knew
That I Had To Love You
From A Distance
I Never Knew That This
Was An' Unconditional Rule
I May Have Said It
Mo' Than Once Or Twice
But I Don't Wanna Be The One
To Mess Up U're Life
As The World Aroun' Us
Is Goin' Insane
I Guess You Know I Never
Played You Like A Game
But I Always Seem To Be
The One To Blame
Once You Come Up Short
Backed Into A Corner Again
Somewhere Between
A Rock An' The Deep Blue Sea
Well I Could Never Be
But You Matta' To Me
Even When Opposites
Learn To Agree
Still They Walk Away
From Their True Destiny

If Its' A Perfect Fit
Like A Hand In A Glove
This Ole' Fashioned Thing
That We Call Modern Love
Well I Guess That The Real Thing
Wasn't Good Enough
Waitin' In The Wings
As We Jus' Pass It Up
So Whatever I Do
You Know Its' True
I'll Always Give You The Props
When The Credit Is Due
Even If I'm Mistaken For A Fool
Well Its' The Only Way
To Say That I Love You.♡

STATE OF MIND

♣♠♣

Maybe Its' True

But I Don't Know

When They Say

All Roads Lead To Rome

As Everybody Tries

To Make It Home

Baby If You Lead

Maybe I Will Follow

Though It Might Be

A Grand Design

To Think This Seventh Heaven

Is Made Of Sunshine

Or Justa' Separation

Of Church An' State

For The Ones You Love

We Will Always Wait

An' You Can Find

This Key There Anytime

To The Door That Unlocks

A Love Divine

But Until That Day

I Will Surely Stay

To Fight Those Demons

All Along The Way

Its' A State Of Mind

For All To See

Could Be A Self-Fulfillin' Prophecy

Or There Could Be Somethin'

Lurkin' In The Dark

A Word To You Lovers

You Betta' Watch U're Hearts.☆

SHADOW OF A DOUBT

Its' Everythin' That You Said

Its' The Voice In My Head

Its' There Every Night

Before I Go To Bed

Its' Not So Easy To Be

When U're Livin' So Lonely

Its' Hard To Realize

U're Not The One An' Only

Sometimes They Turn You Down

Sometimes They Turn You Away

Sometimes They Won't Let You Talk

When You Got Somethin' To Say

Sometimes They Make You Wait

When U're In Need Of A Break

Sometimes They String You Along

Before They Turn You Away

A Double Portion I See

Once You Count Thirty Three

I Guess That's Sixty Six

An' Too Much For Me

Now Its' Me Against The World

Afraid To Take My Turn

Until I Find That Pearl

I Guess The Truth May Burn

Well I Got Knocked To The Groun'

By A Phantom Sucka' Punch

Snookered Into A Corner

By The Stroke Of A Genius

Well It Coulda' Bein' My Skills

Or The Hand Of God

But Still I Made It Through

Without The Shadow Of A Doubt.☆

NAKED TRUTH

♧♤♧

Realize U're Acclimatized
    By The Hypothesis
        Of A Calculation
            Somehow You Didn't Know
                You Were Juxtapose
                    Set Against The Backdrop
                    Of A Bad Situation

Identified An' Serialized
    By A Criminalizing Organization
        On Some Dead End Streets
            Coz You Had Some Beef
                With Some Dropouts
                    Who Had No Education

B'Coz Of The Hype
    You Were Stereotyped
        With U're Swag Attitude
            An' The Garms' U Was Wearin'
            Also The Choice
                An' The Sound Of U're Voice
                Gave You Away
                    B'Coz You Were Swearin'

How Could You Succeed
    After Bunnin' The Weed
        An' Then Declarin' The Streets
            Was Worth Defendin'
                Losin' U're Rights
                    For Takin' A Life
                        Somewhere In A Cell
                            Actin' Up Like Its' Leisure

After The Fame
    Now U're Playin' A Game
        Until U're Contained
            At His Majesty's Pleasure
                Somehow You Didn't Think
                    Or Try To Make The Link
                      Between Breakin' Away
                        An' Now U're Servin'
                        A Sentence

Yeh' You Wanted It Bad
    The Name That You Had
        Not Even Concerned
            About U're Own Reputation
                Beginnin' To Sink
                    Now You Can't Even Think
                    What's Going Down
                      In U're Own Revelation

Thinkin' Its' Cool
    To Have A Bad Attitude
        That's Goin' Aroun'
           The Whole Neighbourhood
              Yeh' Until You Got Served
                Now U're Preaching The Word
                  Yeh' The Whole Damn Truth
                    To The Congregation

Now You Understand
    That The Boy Is A Man
        Despite The Mistakes
           We All Keep On Makin'
              Tryin' To Connect
                An' Still Redirect
                  To Meet With The God
                    Upon U're Salvation

Without A Doubt
    What The Story's About
        Everybody Moved On'
           But U're Still There Prayin'
              Hopin' This Peace
                Can One Day Release You
                  From All Of The Crimes
                    That You Have Committed

The Naked Truth
Is All Around Me
I'll Gladly Repay You
For What I Owe
The Services Rendered
For Entertainment
Well This Must Be
A Hard Act To Follow.☆

PINK AN' BLUE

Fiction Is Stranger

Than You An' Me

In The Soberin' Moments

U're Smellin' The Coffee

Its' Like The Alchemy

From A Pharmacy

From The A.C.M.E

Tradin' Company

Before I Go Down

Into My Grave

I Hope I've Done Enough

To Amend My Ways

Cos Its' Jus' Me An' My Heart

Walkin' In The Dark

Searchin' For The Light

Waitin' For The Spark

U'll Never Understand

Until It Happens To You

An' I Can't Be Justa' Pawn

To See You Through

So If U're Leavin' Me

Jus' Leave Me Alone

Cos I've Made Up My Mind

To Be On My Own

An' All Those Innocent

Boys An' Girls

Are Much Too Precious

To Live In This World

An' All Those Diamonds An' Pearls

Of Every Shade An' Hue

Are Jus' Like The Colours

Of Pink An' Blue. ☆

WHOLE HAPPINESS

However The Lady, Makes Up Her Mind
Can Surely Take Science By Surprise

A Brave New Girl, An' Ordinary World
An' Unconditional Love, But Only On Her Own Terms

Walkin' Out The Door, Leadin' To The Gate
Now She's Takin' The Path, While Destiny Waits

From The Trials Of Life, She's Knows Her ABCs
Now That She's Holdin' The Keys, Of A Great Mystery

Its' Not Jus' Her Faith Or The Things She Believes In
Its' Not That She Sows What Everybody Is Reapin'

She Might Not Seem To Care, If Its' A Waste Of Time
Barefoot An' Beautiful, In The Rays Of The Sunshine

She's Always In Need Of Care An' Affection
She Always Demands U're Undivided Attention

Whatever Her Motives She Might Not Profess
But Heaven Knows Love, Is Her Whole Happiness. ☆

2. द्वा.ሁለት

PSYCOMPOSITIONS

जब्‌बा.የጅቢ जब्‌बा.ጀባ पक्षी.ወፍ

ODD ONE OUT

♣♠♣

I Knocked On The Door

An' It Started To Open

I Was Seekin' The Things

Hopin' To Find

I Asked To Receive

Whatever Was Given

When All Of These Questions

Entered My Mind

Some Go In Search

Of Their Rewards

Layin' Out Their Stalls

Lookin' For Promotions

Some Want The Money

All Of The Gold

But Some Of Us Were Told

To Worship Beside The Altar

Some Have Claimed

To Hear Their Names

Again An' Again

David, Martha An' Matthew

Somewhere Outside

It Started To Rain

On Those Who Proclaim

The Body's A Temple

But Could I Be

The Odd One Out

No Longer The Masta'

Of My Own House

An' Could It Be

A Worthy Cause

All For One

One For All. ☆

SOUL

♣♠♣

So How Can You Own
    What You Don't Own
        Not Even Da' Rights
            To U're Very Own Soul

An' Dare I Not Mention
    In Seekin' Possession
        What Satan Requires
            Without God's Protection

Yeah Heaven Is Waitin'
    U're Jus' On Probation
        Before You Arrive
            At U're Final Destination

Yeah Note 4 Note
    If You Think Its' A Joke
        Somethin' Designed
            In The Bible They Wrote

An' Yet Spoken In Sermons
    To All Of The Vermin
        That Somethin' Inside Of U're Soul
            Was So Certain

A Word Of Advice
    From The Kingdom Of Christ
        For Those Paralysed
            Who Still Want Life

Yeah You Mite' Die Once
    But You Only Live Twice
        But Eternity
            Is Not A Roll Of The Dice

Yeah So How Can You Fake It
    When The Soul Is Still Naked
        Waitin' For God
            Or Satan To Claim It

For The Souls Outside
    My Window Sill
        Yeah Are Using Words
            That Are Designed To Kill

Yeah You Think Its' A Game
    To Be Played By The Rules
        If You Ain't Got A Soul
            Then You Ain't Got A Clue

Yeah Despite All The Flesh
    U've Broken Into
        Yeah I'm Only Talkin' To Souls
        I Ain't Talkin' To You

Its' Not A Personal Thing
        For You To Pick Or Choose
                Its' Jus' A Higher Vibration
                U're Entitled Too

Yeah The More That You Dream
        Is The More You Have Visions
                An' By Definition
                        Its' Jus' Premonitions

For The Motivation
        That's In Control
                Yeah U're Body, U're The Spirit
                Is Guided Soul

So If You Had A Goal
        Then What Would It Be
                Cos If U're Soul Is Blind
                        Then U're Spirit Can't See

Until You See
        That This Reality
                Is Not Everythin'
                        What It Appears To Be
                        Until U're Soul
                                Is Finally Free. ☆

THINGS TO COME
♣♤♣

There Seems To Be

A Lot Of Movin' Parts

Maybe This Could Be

A Contradiction

Somewhere Between

The Head An' The Heart

Only Goes To Show

Why Its' So Complicated

Remember When You Looked

What's Written In That Book

The One That Made You Take

That Hypocritical Oath

As For The Things That Fly

Or Swim In The Sea

They Are None Mo' Separate

Than You An' Me

For Those Who Like To Rise

Simply Fall In Love

As We're Watchin'

It All Fall Apart

So Whoever You Are

Under That Distant Star

I Guess You Know By Now

U're Not The Only One

When There Appears

To Be No End In Sight

Only The Brightest Star

Can Give You Sunlight

An' Even The Blind

Wouldn't Cross That Line

But It Could Be A Sign

Of Things To Come. ☆

NO FAULT OF OUR OWN

♧♤♧

While We Were Divided
By A Spirit Of Love Unrequited

Even When Most Of The Wisest
Were All Surprised By The Unknown

For What Had Become Unacceptable
We Shout An' We Scream Until Its' Permissible

For The Sheddin' Of A Tear An' A Contrite Heart
What Else Would Stop Us Tearin' Ourselves Apart

Like Birds Of A Feather Flockin' Together
Only To Find Out Love Has Flown

Tryin' To Reach The Goal Of An' Ultimate Soul
Has Only Brought Us To Bring Each Other Down

An' For Now It Seems We Can Only Appease Thee
An' Pray To Love As We Beseech Thee

An' For Now It Seems We Are The Needy
Through No Fault Of Our Own

I Guess You Can't Be Blamed
For What You Don't Know. ☆

LINE OF DEFENCE

They Won't Let Me Be

They Won't Let Me Alone

They're Always Bringin' Beef

To My Door

It Seems They Got Da' Lowdown

When I'm Makin' My Moves

It Seems They're Speculatin'

About What I Do

They Wait In Anticipation

When I'm Down On The Block

They're Always Spreadin' Rumours

Like A News Carrier

They Wanna Know My Business

When I'm Out On The Street

They Wanna Know Where I Bein'

An' Whose Bein' With Me

Every Day They' Keep Talkin'

Like They Got Sumpthin' To Say

Every Night They Be Stalkin'

Invadin' My Space

With Nuthin' Betta' To Do

Than Messin' With My Mind

Castin' All Their Stones

As The Blind Keep Leadin' The Blind

I Don't Know Why

They Keep Comin' Roun' Here

But Everyday

I Got To Turn Em' Away

Cos It Could Be

My Last Line Of Defence

But They Always Keep Guessin'

All That I Do Or Say. ☆

WILL NEVER DO

♧♤♧

Was It Jus' My Recollection
Or Jus' The Thoughts Of My Reflections

Watchin' History In Repeat
Jus' For Me To Suffer This Defeat

Somehow These Memories Of My Lonely Condition
Becomes The Guilty State Of My Convictions

What Did I Squander In Vain, Jus' By Learnin' This Game
Judgin' By These Rules I Wouldn't Wanna Play

For The Shortest Time When I Was In U're Presence
Was It Jus' For Me To Learn All The Lessons

Was It Jus' A Taste Of What It Could Be
Jus' Anotha' Life, Remotely An' Briefly

An' No Matta' The Fate I've Fallen Into
Love Put Me Under This Spell, Now I'm Broken In Two

An' No Matta' The Reasons, Whatever I Choose
It Seems To Be That The One Will Never Do. ☆

STONE THE CROWS

♣♠♣

A Writer Takes His Pen

Tells The Story Again

A Damsel In Distress

Waitin' For A Hero

A Sailor On The Seas

A New Discovery

A Land Of Mystery

Where The Waters Are Flowin'

The Water Takes Its' Course

Towards A Waterfall

I Watch The River Flow

Into The Sea

What Took So Many Years

For Me To Face My Fears

Now That My Lonely Tears

Are Runnin' Into Streams

You Know I Waited Six Days

But On The Seventh I Sailed

I Was Goin' In Search

Of The Holy Grail

But As I Drifted Thru'

The River Brought Me To You

The Waterfall That I Knew

Was My Happy Tears

An' It Was You After All

Takin' Me By Surprise

My God Well Stone The Crows

An' It Was True After All

Why Its' Taken So Long

For Me To Get Back Home. ☆

REALITY
(INEVITABLE BEING)

There's A New World Emergin'
    From Jus' Beyond The Window Curtain

An' I'm Certain There Mus' Be
    A Supreme Inevitable Being

My Reflection' Upon The Water
    The Moon An' The Stars Have Surely Altered

From The Natural Order That I Perceive
    From The Supreme Inevitable Being

When A New Day Is Arisin'
    An' We Welcome The Sun Upon The Horizon

Wakin' Up From Our Sleep Only To Be Greeted
    By The Supreme Inevitable Being

An' All Of My Worries Seem To Be
    Such A Trouble An' Strife Botherin' Me

An' I Wonder If God Can Really See
    The Condition Of My Reality. ☆

RAISON D'ETRE

For All Of The Things

I Was Denied

I Never Stop Believin'

I Never Stop Tryin'

But I Hoped One Day

That There Would Come A Time

To Satisfy This Feelin'

To Fulfil My Desires

For The Blemishes

That I Try To Hide

Still Its' All Transparent

Inside Of My Mind

Ever Since The Days

Of My Conception

There's Only One Story

I Keep On Tellin'

Nightmares Come

An' Demons Know

That This Is A Battle

For The Soul

As They Rattle My Cage

But I Keep On Dreamin'

A Fight For The Right

To Justify Why I'm Breathin'

Despite Being Made

Of Clay An' Dust

My Only Reasons For Livin'

Was My Wanderlust

An' If There's Nothin' Else

That I Could Be

This Is My Raison D'etre

My Only Reasons For Being. ☆

OUTER SPACE

♧♤♧

The Totem-Pole Of Red, White An' Blue
Is Full Of Activism An' Climate Hysteria

An' All The Colours Of Red, Gold An' Green
Represents The Flag Of U're Eco-Fever

An' All The Local Superheroes
Somewhere On Earth 616

Have Traded In Their Flyin' Capes
Becomin' Demonstrators, Amongst The Riotin'

He's A Walkin' Talkin' Tickin' Timebomb
In A Spandex Straight Jacket, Tied An' Restrained

With His Toe Cap Boots An' Uniform On
He's Suited An' Booted, He's Part Of The Parade

I Know The End Is Out Of Sight
Somehow We Were Told About The Humble Beginnins'

In This Dictionary P.C World
There's Always Wanna' Stick You Whenever U're Winnin'

For The Greatest Ambitions Of U're Tiny Mind
Expandin' Throughout Our Universe

As The Gravity Comes Crashin' Down
An' Mankind Returns To Outer Space. ☆

SCREWS ON THE BLUES

♧♤♧

Nuthin' Mo' Social

Than A Free Society

Nuthin' Mo' Religious

Than The Truth Settin' You Free

Nuthin' Like The Rules

Of The Governin' Government

Nuthin' Like The Policy

Of Anotha' Political Stunt'

Its' Hard To Wake Em' Up

When They're Livin' Inside A Dream

Its' Hard To Shake Em' Up

With A Regula' Cup Of Coffee

Its' Almost Disbelief

While They're Starin' At The Screen

Could Be A Storm In A Teacup

Or Jus' A Lowdown Dirty Scheme

The Greatest Revelation

The Revolution Is Now

From U're Front Row Seat

You See What's Goin' Down

Could Be Anotha' Protest

Tearin' Up These Streets

Now Its' All Over Town

With Commercial Breaks In-Between

Scandals In The Papers

Headlines On The News

The Latest Breakin' Story

They Got The Screws On The Blues

The Information Highway

Nobody Seems To Know

The Blues Is On The Lowdown

But Which Way Will They Go. ☆

THE GAME

♧♤♧

They Always Say Its' Fair Play
When U're Risin' Up To Meet With Fame

So When You Reach The Very Top
Keep Lookin' Up, Don't Ever Stop

You Thought That I Was Destined To Fail
When I Found Myself In This Livin' Hell

Fightin' Harda' To Prevail
Until I Learned The Rules Of Engagement

You Might Be The First, To End Up Last
Against The Tumbleweed An' All The Crickets

But What Can You Do, If You Leave It To Chance
The Chaff An' The Wheat, Suffer The Harvest

As All The Victors Are Standin' Proud
The Underdogs An' All The Winners

You Know The Game Is Over Now
For All Of The Clowns An' All Of The Losers. ☆

MISFITS AN' WEIRDOS

♧♤♧

Have I Got News For You

I Got It From The Muse

The Clues From Dr. Zeus

Recently Appointed

I Hear Them Makin' Some Claims

Though Some Say Not In My Name

I Guess This Topic Of Discussion

Ain't Worth Debatin'

They're Watchin' What You Do

The Cameras Pointed At You

You Gotta' Be Teflon Proof

With A Good Alibi

You Jus' Can't Make It Up

The Truth Is Never Enough

But Somethin' Might Erupt

At The Scene Of The Crime

Its' All Bein' Sanitized

Brainwashed An' Analyzed

Not That Its' Verified

I Guess U're Good To Go

But Don't Be

Changin' U're Stations

Or Adjustin' Race Relations

Could Be A Technical Glitch

But The Problems Bein' Solved

Somehow These

Misfits An' Weirdos

Have Taken Control

Waltzin' Thru' The Halls

An' Down Corridors

I Guess These

Misfits An' Weirdos

Makin' Fools Of Us All

By Runnin' The World

From The Notes On A Postcard. ☆

DELIRIUM & DESPAIR

I'm Jus' The Latest Captain Chaos

Emergin' From A Disaster Zone

Some May Say A Occupational Hazard

Mo' Than You Can Imagine

I Think You Ought To Know

It Could Be A Case Of Psychiatry

For Me To Figure Out What I'm Livin' For

Swallowin' On That Bitta' Pill

Jus' For Me To Function

An' Overdose Of Consumption

Despite The Insanity Of My Reality

I Guess You Could Say That I'm Insecure

Still I'm Hangin' On To The Edge Of My Seat

So Unawares That I'm Losin' Control

Somewhere In-Between Delirium An' Despair

I Guess I'm Not Accustomed To Be Livin' Out-There

I Know The Love In My Mind Might Be Colour-Blind

But I'm Jus' Tryin' To Find A Love Of My Own. ☆

LOVE IS ALKALINE

♧♤♧

What I Seem To Need Is Killin' Me
An' My Beliefs In Spirituality

Whatever It Is That I Conceive
Is Hard To Achieve In My Destiny

I Know That U're Love Is Alkaline
But Still We Enhance One Anotha'

I Know That U're Passions Are Deep Inside
But Still I Know It Burns Like A Phire

I Won't Put Up A Front To Get What I Want
Still I Recognise There's Much Mo' To Me

So Why Call It A Game By Any Otha' Name
When Its' Plain To See U're My Destiny

I Know U're Desires Are Somethin' Divine
It Only Yearns To Take You Much Higha'

I Know U're Spirit's An' Unbridled Flame
Makin' My Life So Much Brighta'

Whatever The Dream Of My Reality
That Was The Way That It Should Be

Whatever I Know, Wherever I Go
I Know U're Bound To Follow So Desperately. ☆

THE LAYMAN

♣♠♣

A Dreadful Night In Hades

3 Mo' Days In Hell

I Won't Talk About My Life

Cos I Know Where I've Bein'

Bedevilled An' Confused

Unjustly Crucified

The Dictates Of A Muse

Weighs Heavy On My Mind

Potions An' Concoctions

Whiskey Turned Into Wine

Inferior Inhibitions

I Feel My Confidence Rise

Like Those Cavemen Brawlin'

In The Dead Of The Night

Well You Can Call Me A Coward

For Refusin' To Fight

Amongst The Horny Flowers

The Thistles An' The Weeds

I'm Scared Of All My Fears

Uprootin' Humanity

Anotha' Nightmare Movie

Anotha' Hollywood Dream

Of Silent Voices Screamin'

Subtitles On A Screen

The Layman In His Terms

Is Preachin' Prose An' Poetry

To The Anointed Fans

Conscripts With Their Beliefs. ☆

UNFORGIVABLE SINS
(HOLY GHOST)

You Know That I'm Bold
When I'm Weak

You Know That I'm Straight
As A Freak

An' Indulgent Mind
Of Imagination

With Nuthin' To Replace
A State Of Salvation

You Know My Soul
Is Incomplete

The Loss An' Defeats
A Life On The Streets

Still You Taught Me
Who I Should Glorify

Its' Why I Never Hide
From The Wink In U're Eye

Of All The Things
    I Chose To Believe

      I Guess I Never Dreamt
        That I Could Be Deceived

An' Yet This Phony Hubris
    Takes Another Disguise

      But Its' You That I Turn Too
        In These Troubled Times

You Know The Places
    That I've Bein'

      Everythin' About Me
        My Unforgivable Sins

You Know My Heart
    What's Written Within'

      How The Story Began
        How My Life Will End. ☆

THE SUN

♧♤♧

Eyes, Realise

The Camera Never Lies

Love, Forever Is Blind

I Guess That's Why

I Never See You In Dreams

I've Always Seen

Places I've Never Been Too

But I Know

Way Down In My Soul

Those Are The Places

I Wanna Go With You

Alone An' Remote

I Find It Hard To Cope

An' Hope Is Jus' A Word

That I Cling Onto

An' This Life That I Live

Is All I Have To Give

Waitin' For Somethin'

Or Someone To Show You

When Black Turns To White

An' Day Turns To Night

When There's No One

No One In Sight

Left To Call Out Too

When The Rain

An' Thunder Comes

An' You Go Lookin'

For The One

I Guess It Coulda Bein'

So Much Fun

Instead Of Sittin' Here

Starin' At The Sun. ☆

FORBIDDEN FRUIT

♧♤♧

Do You Agree With Me
This Is How The Other Half Lives
Could It Be Eroticism
Is Always Seduced By Promises
If Temptation, Is So Wrong
Well Its' No Wonder, Why Sin Exist
Could It Be Jones Versus Jones
Or Another Case Of Mister Or Miss
Of All The Plants, We've Come To Know
There's A Flower That Grows
In Solomon's Garden
A Medicinal Herb, A Harvest To Reap
To Help You Sleep
While The Willow Is Weeping
We've Come To Know
What We've Never Known
We've Come To Learn
We're Only Naked
An' Now You See Reality
From The Knowledge Tree
Was Far From Perfect
I Guess You Wasn't Meant For Me
I Guess I Wasn't Meant For You
A Total Eclipse Of The Heart
The Sweetest Taste Of Forbidden Fruit. ☆

SELL BY DATE
♧♤♧

Guess You Thought You Could Win

So You Went Back Again

Caught Up In The Middle

Of A Smokescreen

All You Latecomers Too

Thought You Could Never Lose

Takin' The Short Cut

Dodgin' The Rules

Like A Fish On The Wire

Wriggle All You Like

But That's What You Get

For Takin' The Biggest Bite

You Can Turn Back Now

While You Still Got Time

Now That U've Come

To The End Of The Line

What's The Quickest Way

Heaven Today

If You Ain't Got No Keys

You Betta' Start Prayin'

All Of You At The Gate

Left It Kinda' Late

Don't You Know That U're Past

U're Sell By Date. ☆

LIVE

♣♠♣

We Both Want The Same Things
Sometimes We Wanna Change Things
Sometimes We Jus' Wanna Blame Somebody Else
Sometimes We Want Affection
An' Feel The Same Connection
Go In The Same Direction
The Way That We Came
When I Think That I'm Fallin'
You Know Its' You That I'm Callin'
So Baby Please Stop Stallin'
An' Pick Up The Phone
Were At The Point Of The Rescue
When Broken Hearts Seem To Bleed Through
Baby All Of The Pain We've Ever Known
Sometimes I Jus' Wanna Hold You
Not In A Way To Control You
Sometimes I Jus' Don't Know
But It Seems Like We've Changed
Throughout The Day An' The Night Time
Sometimes We Find The Right Time
To Keep Our Spirits Up
Before We Lay Down Low
Tell Me What It Is, Tell Me What It Is
Tell Me What It Is, Jus' To Love An' Live. ☆

NO WAY OUT

The Cost Of Living

In Broken Britain

The Capitalism

Of Hand To Mouth

The Peaceful Missions

The Stop The War Coalition

The Globalism

As Empires Rise

The Rough Conditions

Of People In Prisons

A Search For The Missing

Is Now Nationwide

The Cities On Lockdown

The Drug Bust Crackdown

The Addiction Of Afflictions

An' Suicides

The Hike Up Of Prices

The Strikers In Their Crisis

The Screws An' All The Vices

Keepin' Us Down

The Youths In Their Aggression

In A Deeper Depression

The Violence An' Oppression

Is All Around

No Voice For The Lonely

To Avoid All The Only

People Who Have Told Me

There's No Way Out

No Faith To Believe In

We're Just Facing Our Demons

Still Everybody's Screaming

There's No Way Out. ☆

AGAPE
(NO RESPECTER OF PERSONS)

Movers An' Shakers Callin' The Shots
They Got The Puppets Below, Puppet Masters Up Top
U're Playin' The Game, Straight Into Their Hands
Nuthin' Short Of Illegal, But This Is The Plan

A Man In Uniform Of Gold An' Brass
A Cross An' A Book, A Gun An' A Badge
Whatever The Story U're Willin' To Sell
The Only Choice You Got Between Heaven An' Hell

As Much As I Know, Life Isn't So Fair
Somebody To Watch, Somebody To Care
Whatever It Is, I Take It Right There
Wherever U're Going, I'm Goin' Somewhere

You Might Need A Sense Of Humour
Before They Start To Read You U're Last Rites
B'Cos I Know Its' Not A Laughin' Matta'
Its' Mo' Than A Joke When U're In Need Of Hope

Its' Like A Russian Roulette
Between The Black An' The Red
Somebody Wins, Somebody Winds Up Dead
I'm No Respecter Of Persons, But I Treat You The Same
I Know The Word Is Egalian
I Know The Word Is Agape. ☆

TEARS YOU DOWN

There's Something In The Sky

Jus' Beginning To Fly

I've Seen It With My Eyes

The Devil Tears It Down

The Tears I Use To Cry

Afraid That I Would Die

Way Before My Time

The Devil Tears Me Down

There's Something You Should Know

About This Haunted Soul

Wherever It May Go

The Devil Tears You Down

The War Inside U're Mind

U're Fighting All The Time

You Haven't Figured Out Why

The Devil Tears You Down

The Children Of This Earth

You Don't Know What U're Worth

Since God Gave You Birth

The Devil Tears You Down

U're Daughters An' U're Sons

They're Not The Only Ones

Cos When U're Kingdom Comes

The Devil Tears It Down

It Might Be Complimentary

An' It Might Feel Comfortable

An' It Could Be A Pack Of Lies

But It Always Sounds Like The Truth. ☆

DISTRACTION

♧♤♧

The Higher They Climb, Jus' To Undermine

Somethin' Designed, Like The Tower Of Babel

Denying The Proof, Uprootin' The Truth

Until History Is Completely Irrelevant

Like A Pack Of Wolves, They Turned On You

Even Though They Knew, You Were Never Against Them

Hidin' Their Vices Within Plain Sight

While Makin You A Victim Of Their Crimes

An' All Of The While, The Vitriolic An' Vile

Are Pourin' They're Scorn

Upon The Guileless, An' Innocent

With Inverted Smiles Til All Is Defiled

As They Smother Everything Born Of Spiritual Reverence

An' Yet The Intellect Beyond The Dark Net

Is Spawnin' A Life Of Imitation

An' The Light That Shines Illuminates Our Dreams

As Great As It Seems, Its' Jus' Another Distraction. ☆

FREEDOM
♣♤♣

There's Nothing On Offer

At My Corner Store

I Guess Its' The Same Things

As The Day Before

I'm Sorry I Put You

Through All Of Those Things

I'm Sorry I Hurt You

For No Good Reason

Guess I Couldn't See

What Was Wrong With Me

There Was Someone Else

I Was Tryin' To Be

But U're My Guardian Angel

U're The Muse In The Sky

U're Always In My Head

U're Always In My Mind

They Would Never Be Fair

I Could Never Be True

Coz The Fairness In Truth

Only Makes Me A Fool

I Need You Mo' Than Wishes

I Wish I Didn't Need You At All

If Wishes Are Never Granted

Then What Are Wishes For

Freedom From Pressure

Freedom From Pain

Freedom To Drive

Somewhere Down The Freeway

Freedom For You

Freedom For Me

The Freedom Of Life

Is All That We Need. ☆

PERHAPS

♣♤♣

Last Night I Laid Down With The Blues
Woke Up This Mornin', Feelin' The Same Way Too

Seems I Was Feelin' Kinda Confused
I Thought About You

Perhaps You Can Make Me Forget
All Of The Things That I Regret

Once I Finally Paid Off My Debts
To This Society

Way Off Limits, Love Is Out Of Fashion
Somehow It Seems To Be A Crime

Still I'm Watchin' All The Lonely People
Walkin' In Straight Lines

Perhaps You Can Ease The Burden
That's Bein' Heavy On My Mind

Before The Act Of The Final Curtain
Takes Away My Sunshine

Seems Like These Dogs Are Always Barkin'
About These Gods Of London Town

Without A Bone To Pick Me Up
It Seems Like They're Ready, To Put Me Down

Perhaps You Have Got Me Mixed Up
Caught Up In A Fix With Some Other Guy

But Right Now I Need A Good Tip
So I Don't Waste U're Precious Time. ☆

NEW LEAF

♧♤♧

I'm Puttin' My Foot Down

On This Solid Groun'

I Only Need The Sound

Of My Heartbeat

I Ain't Chasin' Time

Or Simply Towin' The Line

I Paid Up All My Dues

To Get What's Mine

No Matta' What They Say

I'm Still Walkin' Away

I Can't Depend Upon

All My Yesterdays

Coz It Feels Like A Trap

Somethin' That's Holdin' Me Back

I Won't Look Over My Shoulda'

To Recover My Tracks

I Won't Be Lookin' Aroun'

Caught In The Lost An' Found

I've Had Enough Of This Life

Keepin' Me Down

You Might Call It Fate

But It Only Gets In The Way

I'm Jus' Lookin' Ahead

To A Bran' New Day

I'm Turnin' Over A New Leaf

I'm Tired Of The Things That's Needlin' Me

I've Had Enough Of Losin' Sleep

I'm Turnin' Over A New Leaf. ☆

FOOD CHAIN
(RIGHTEOUS PATH)
♣♠♣

Higher Up On The Food Chain

Don't You Know Somebody's

Gonna Bite U're Head Off

Higher Up On The Food Chain

Don't You Know Somebody's

Gonna Eat U're Heart Out

You Betta' Watch Where U're Goin'

You Betta' Watch What U're Sowin'

The Way That This Is Flowin'

Karma's Comin' Aroun'

Its' Jus' The Law Of The Jungle

Even Though We Might Stumble

A Lesson For The Humble

On That Righteous Path

Lower Down On The Chain Gang

Don't You Know Somebody's

Gonna Put You In Bondage

Lower Down On The Chain Gang

Don't You Know That Life's

A Little Too Hard To Manage

For The Meek An' The Weakest

A Struggle For Existence

Survival Of The Fittest

On That Righteous Path. ☆

KNOWLEDGE

Catch 22, Not Good Enough For You

I Guess We Know The Score, Its' Catch 44

Funny But True, Now I'm Invisible

Ain't It Funny How People Look Straight Through You

You Got Me Wrong, So I Wrote This Song

An' I Don't Need To Belong, If I'm Not Accepted

Stranger Than Faith, How Do You Get Saved

If The Way You Behave, Is Rejected

Mo' Recently I've Noticed In Me

That U're Takin' Note Of My Appearance

But Why Should I Hide, If I've Bein Cast Aside

Why Should I Change My Direction

No One I Know, I Am Nothing

Knowledge I Know, I Have No Ledge. ☆

LITTLE ANT
♧♤♧

Well I've Got Me

Some Solutions

But I Got No Time

To Solve It

Well I Know

Its' An' Awkward Situation

That's Causin' Me

Too Many Problems

Well This Must Be

My Last Meal

My Farewell

Before The Inquisition

Before They Hang Me

Out To Dry

My Only Crime

Is Wishful Thinkin'

Well Its' Me

An' My Idiosyncrasies

With My Cogimabits

On A Shoppin' Spree

Now That You Got The Choice

You Don't Need To Choose

The Cheerleaders In The Back

Will Brighten Up The Room

I Wasn't Much Bigga'

Than A Little Ant

Jus' Tryin' To Make A Noise

Like An Elephant

Well I Was Comin' Up

With The Sun Goin' Down

I Was Part Of The Circus

Rollin' Into Town. ☆

THE DEAL

♧♤♧

Findin' You Was Highly Unlikely
It Was Mo' Like Improbable
On A Scale Of 1 To 100
I Guess It Was Mo' Like Unpredictable

Sometimes Its' Hard
To Balance The Scales
Though You Try To Win
You Know You Often Fail

Its' Either This Or That
Between The Red An' The Black
But Everythin' I Had
I Bet It All On You

I'm Only Speculatin'
Between What's Right An' Wrong
But In This Numbers Game
I Think I Left It Too Long

Tell Me What Did I Miss
In My Hypothesis
If It Comes Down To Luck
Tell Me Why Should I Quit

I Think The Law Of Averages
Could Never Be True
Well That Was Until
I Ran Into You

Despite What I Know,
Despite What I Feel
Losin' You
Wasn't Part Of The Deal. ☆

PLANS TO LEAVE

♣♠♣

Beneath The Gaze Of A Lazy Horizon

Where The Moon Meets The Sun

The Exploration Of An Invitation

Without A Compass, A Map Or A Chart

Across The Sea, The Scenery

I See The Mountains An' The Trees

Well There Was A Time When I Knew

This Country From A Different Point Of View

Far Away From A Familiar Place

Somewhere Lost In Paradise

A Breakaway, Faraway Excursion

Daydreamin' The Nights Somewhere In Flight

I'm Always Makin' Plans To Leave

But My Body Won't Let Me Go

I'm Always Thinkin' Of Ways To Be Free

But Nobody Told My Heart An' Soul. ☆

ONE AN' ALL

♧♤♧

The Devil Is A Man Who's Jus' Misunderstood
Love Is Jus' A Language For The Common Good
Now Heaven's A Destination Waitin' To Be Reached
By Those In Anticipation Willin' To Seek

The Future Is A Place, Everybody Can Dream
The Future Is A Place, Where Nobody Has Been
It Can Take The Words Right Out Of U're Mouth
It Can Almost Surprise You
It Can Make You Scream An' Shout

You Can Open A Book For Interpretations
You Can Open A Book, But There's Only One Version
Well It Might Be This An' It Might Be That
No Matter How You Separate
All The Truth From The Facts

Its' Jus' A Waste Of Time Talkin' To The Blind
Until The God Inside Has Opened U're Eyes
Consider This If Any Its' Not For The Many
But I'm Sure You'll Agree There Must Be Plenty
For One An' All. ☆

UNEXPECTED

♣♠♣

Some Debts

Are Never Paid

Some Mistakes

Are Never Corrected

Some Lies

Are Hard To Believe

Some Stories Told

Are Only One-Sided

Some Souls

Are Hard To Redeem

Some People Can Dream Things

They've Never Seen

Some Hearts

Are Broken Apart

Some People Never Heal

They Jus' Keep On Driftin'

Some People Like You

Some People Like Me

Learn To Disagree

They Learn To Bury The Hatchet

But We Both Know

What The Points Are For

It Doesn't Matter Who Scored

As Long As We're Both Winnin'

So I'm Gonna Love You

Not Like Before

Not Like The Time

When You Close The Door

We Both Know The Game

We've Already Played

But People Can Change

Unexpected. ☆

GOOD ENOUGH
♧♤♧

I Guess There's No Other Way

To Reach A Compromise

If Its' Only These Lies

Keeping Us As Allies

Somehow This Family Dream

Has Almost Got Me Knee Deep

Diggin' My Way Out

Of This Abject Poverty

Now Its' You That I Find

Was Being Less Than Kind

By Simply Pulling The Wool

Right Over My Eyes

I Guess You Hide Behind

What You Put Up Front

Maybe In Trying To Be Good

I'm Just Not Good Enough. ☆

WISHIN' WELL

♣♠♣

If You Were Me An' I Was You
Is There Anything Different
That We Would Do
If The Choice To Choose
Between Life An' Death
A Set Of Hollow Rules
That We Were Bound.To Break
Upon U're Head, Upon U're Hand
Upon U're Marks, Get Ready An' Set U're Path
As We Excel Towards The End
With No Code Or Principles Left To Defend
For Those Who Wait
To Lay Their Weapons Down
Surely Carry The Burden
Of Their Ancestors Now
A Steppin' Stone Of Broken Bones
A Shallow Grave That Guides You Home
If There's No Mo' Wishes
In U're Wishin' Well
Now There's Nuthin' To Buy
An' Nuthin' To Sell
An' For Those Who Preach
An' Proclaim In Vain
There's Nuthin' Left To Teach
There's Nuthin' Left To Explain. ☆

DAYS OF OUR YOUTH

♧♤♧

The City Scene

Of A Teenage Dream

Could Only Be

Neon Lights An' Music

Dreamers By Day

Til The Moonlight Came

We Ventured Out

We Went Explorin'

The Love An' Romance

Would Lead Us By Chance

Into The Dance

Into Euphoria

We Went Out On The Streets

6 Days A Week

With One Day For Sleep

But The Pot Was Always Cookin'

We Fell In Love

With The Night Time Buzz

Recreational Drugs

Took Us Higher Than Monuments

We Got Stoned

Walkin' Streets In The Cold

The Club Life

Was Full Of Excitement

The Days Of Our Youth

Were Invincible

We Had No Fears

We Lived For The Glory

The Days Of Our Youth

We Always Knew

It Was Simple An' Cool

An' This Was Our Story. ☆

RAMBLIN' MAN

♧♤♧

I'm A Ramblin' Man
Cigarettes In My Hand

Going From Door To Door
Like An' Insurance Salesman

I'm Filling In Time
By Selling You Sunshine

Jus' In Case You Get Fucked
Out Of Existence

I'm A Ramblin' Man
I'll Help You If I Can

I Got A Payment Plan
For U're Debt Collection

I Got What You Want
I Got What You Need

I Got A Discount On Premiums
I Can Give You For Free

I'm A Ramblin Man
I'm Sure You Understand

If You Can Pay Me In Cash
I'll Make A Reservation

Just Help Me Take Off My Coat
An' Pour A Drink For My Throat

Nobody Needs To Know
We Can Keep It A Secret

I Quote A Really Good Price
I'll Guarantee You For Life

An' If You Need My Advice
Its' Part Of The Package. ☆

SPIRIT RESIDIN'

♣♤♣

Since The Beginnin'

Of Creation

Beyond The Reaches

Of All Explanations

An' The Mysteries

We Were Left To Find

Throughout The Ages

Of Our Time

Now It Seems This World

Is Surely Dyin'

But That's No Reason

To Start Cryin'

As The Truth Before

Was Only Tryin'

To Save U're Life

Of All The Things

That I'd Like To Mention

Beyond The Depths

Of All Comprehension

I'm Only Thinkin' Of

Redemption In Paradise

There's A Beat

Inside Of U're Heart

There's A Thought

Inside Of U're Mind

There's A Place Where You

Set U're Sights

Upon The Horizon

But If We Don't Care At All

Then How Could

We Ever Know

The Secrets Deep

Inside Of U're Soul

Bears The Faith An' Hope

Of A Spirit Residin'. ☆

FACIN' THE WALL

♧♤♧

I Guess You Went To So Much Trouble
To Save Me From Myself
An' Now U're Takin' Me Down A Path
To Start My Journey Again

Does A Baby Cry Coz Its' Afraid To Die
Now I'm Crying All Over Again
From The Sentiments Of What U've Described
Is Something To Hard To Comprehend

Most People Always Seem To Follow
What's Hollow Inside
Most Of Us Always Seem To Borrow
Somebody Else's Time

An' Its' No Wonder Why, We Have To Hide
Afraid Of Pickin' Sides
An' Its' No Matter How Hard We Try
Were Only Victims Of Our Own Crimes

An' We Could Never Be Free Of Possession
Til We Lose Everything We Have
An' Would Anybody Hear Our Confession
Instead Of Talkin' To Ourselves

The Contradiction Of Our Affliction
Is To Blame Everyone Else
The Insanity Of This Humanity
Has Left Us Trapped Inside A Cage

So When U're Breakin' Out
Is When You Start Breakin' Free
I Hope You'll Come An' Find Me
Coz I'll Be Waitin LIke U're Destiny

Now I'm Facin' The Wall
Now I'm Facin' The War
Now I'm Facin' The World
Like Never Before. ☆

HARD TO SEE

♣♤♣

Only A Fool
Can Play This Game Twice

Only A Fool Could
Thinks He's Gonna Get It Right

Now I'm Left To Think
About Everything Else

When All You Ever Thought About
Was U'reself

So You Take Advantage
Not To Be Alone

An' Everybody Thinks
What Everybody Knows

Before You Cash It In
They Stake A Claim On U're Soul

Or Jus' Some Other Fool
Who Wants To Take You Home

I Guess Half Of Love
Would Never Do

A Piece Of Me
A Part Of You

An' For Every Day
That You Walked Away

Each An' Every Night
I Always Forgave

An' After All This Time
When You Come Back To Me

When It Could Never Be
What Its' Suppose To Be

I Guess You Wanna Be Loved
I Guess You Wanna Be Free

What's Too Hard To Understand
Is Too Hard To See. ☆

FREQUENCY

♧♤♧

It Seems U're Too Young To Understand
That You Hold The Fate Of This World In U're Hands

If I Only Knew Then What I Know Now
Wish I Could Find A Way To Tell You Somehow

No Matter Where You Go In This Life
The Bogey Man Always Gets You Right On Time

Remindin' You Of Those Past Lives
The Ones U've Lived, The Ones U've Sacrificed

I Kinda' Found Myself In U're Nick Of The Woods
An' I Bein' Watchin' You But U're Up To No Good

An' All This Hit N' Run You Had U're Kicks For Fun
An' Then U're Gone, An' I'm Alll Alone

She Goes An' She Comes, She Comes An' She Goes
An' That's The Way She Likes It I Suppose

We've Fallen In Love, An' Now Were Startin' To Rise
Except For The Tears, Well Its' A Nice Surprise

But There's Somebody Sleeping In My Bed
An' God Only Knows She Ain't Sleeping With Me

An' The T.Vs Puttin' Ideas Into My Head
Until I Turn Up The Radio To Another Frequency. ☆

PROPULSION

⚜♤⚜

Should A Man Move Faster

Than His Feet Could Carry Him

Is The Future Any Closer

Than The Past Of Yesteryear

If A Man Was Meant To Fly

Why Was He Born Without Wings

If He Can Crawl If He Can Climb

If He Can Do Impossible Things

An' I May Be Upside Down

But I Still Got My Feet On The Ground

Even Though My Head Is In The Clouds

I'm Jus' Floatin Aroun' While I'm Lookin' Down

I Got Speed In My Veins

I Got Propulsion To Accelerate

An' I Got Time In My Hands

I Got Locomotion

An' I'm About To Expand. ☆

DUCKS
(ARE ALL IN A ROW)

♧♤♧

There Is A Story Inside A Book
That I Dreamt Once Before

There Are Pieces Of A Puzzle
That Don't Seem To Fit Anymore

An' If I Loved You Any Less
I Couldn't Miss You Any More

Now This Heart Must Follow A Solitary Path
Upon A Runaway Train Til I Get Home

Well I Think Its' Time For Me To Walk The Line
Forget About The Love That I Left Behind

Until I Find Another You
I Guess The Words An' Music Have To See Me Through

Messages Of Emotion
Strikes A Chord, An' Writes The Page

An' Now U're Ducks Are All In A Row
But Nobody Knows How To Play U're Game. ☆

SHORTEST STRAW

♣♠♣

This Make Believe

Is All We See

An' Everybody

Thinks Its' Real

As We Imitate

The Art We Recreate

As Nature Has Fallen

Into Decay

There's No Pretendin'

How This World Is Endin'

I Guess The Big Bang Theory

Is Jus' A Mushroom Cloud

An' Yet It Could Have Bein'

So Beautiful

Except That We Know

What We Knew Not Somehow

For Those Who Dream

Have Never Seen

How Reality Is So Surreal

I Guess That The Good Times

Wasn't Enough

Jus' To See The Future

For What It Was

An' So This Horizon

Has Nearly Gone

Leavin' Me In Contempt

With The Risin' Sun

So How Can I Pray

For Anotha' Day

If Its' Only Gonna Lead Me

Into Old Age

The End Of An' Age

The End Of A Day

Is All They Could Want

To Ever See

An' If Ever There Was

A Reason To Cry

Its' Hard To Change U're Mind

After U've Died

I Must Have Drawn

The Shortest Straw

But Jus' How Long

Is A Piece Of String

I'm Crawlin' Aroun'

Like Crabs In A Barrel

I Guess I Was

The First One To Blink. ☆

DISINFORMATION

♧♤♧

Now Is The Time
To Call Up A Locksmith
As The Government Decides
To Put Us Boxes
Now U're Freedom Is Dyin'
Cryin' Out Loud
Still You Cannot See Why
They're Controllin' The Crowd
Now You Discover
To Reap U're Bread An' Butter
You Have To Watch The Others Suffer
With An' Open Mind
An' Yet No One Here Is Responsible
Or Why This System Is So Cruel
An' Yet Pretends To Be Kind
Now This Egotistical Society
With A Toxic Culture Is Full Of Enmity
An' Its' No Wonder
Why People Can't Breathe
Or Even Begin To Set Their Minds Free
From The Disinformation Of U're Disclosure
An' The Reasons Why
You Cannot Speak Up Now
From The Gaslitin' Of A Cancel Culture
Meanwhile The Gaggin' Orders
Have Come To Shut You Down. ☆

FIRST IMPRESSIONS
(THE QUIET ONES)

There Was Someone I Use To Know
    But That Was Such A Long Time Ago

        An' You Remind Of A Place An' Time
            The Same Expression Comes To Mind

Well I Guess U've Heard It All Before,
    I Guess I Don't Really Need To Tell You Mo'

        They Say That Lightnin' Never Strikes Twice
            But Its' Hard For Me To Take My Own Advice

It Could Be That Maybe We Met Before
    In Anotha' Lifetime But Who's To Know

        But Even If We Never Meet Again
            Well I Hope You Get There In The End

First Impressions Always Count
    It Lets You Know What Its' All About

        Its' Always The Quiet Ones That You Will Find
            Always Seem To Have Somethin' To Hide. ☆

HIS MASTERS VOICE

They Don't Call It The Ole' Skool

Without A Reason

They Don't Call It A New Style

Cos' Its' Always In Season

We Can Do It Again

But Its' Bein' Done Before

Originality Is Always Keepin' Score

In A World Of Illusions

Its' Always Harda' To Find

Breakin' Out Of The Box

It Takes One Of A Kind

Could Be The Real McCoy

Could Be A Fantasy

But Whatever It Is

It Ain't So New To Me

Some Call It A Craze

Some Call It A Fever

Some Call It A Buzz

Anotha' New Sensation

Some Say Its' A Blast

Rippin' Through This Town

Some Call It Addiction

Its' Happenin' Right Now

An' The Dogs Are Gonna

Chase The Cats

But The Cats

Won't Dance To That

An' The Rats

Are Gettin' Down

In The Back, Listenin'

To His Masters Voice. ☆

CROWD

I'm Not Lookin' For Anyone, No Ones Lookin' For Me
An' That's The Way, Its' Gonna Be

I Paid My Dues I've Even Played The Blues
I Paid My Money For These Bran New Shoes

I'm Not Thinkin' Of Anyone, No Ones Thinkin' Of Me
An' I Don't Need This Selfish Reality

I've Paid The Price I've Even Earned My Stripes
So Don't You Lock Me Up An' Throw Away The Key

I'm Not Missin' Anyone, No Ones Missin' Me
An' I Don't Need U're Loneliness For Company

I've Done My Time, An' Laid It On The Line
Why Don't You Take What's U'res An' Simply Let Me Be

I'm Goin' Down, Way Downtown
Jus' To Lose Myself, Inside This Crowd. ☆

ALMS & TITHES

♣♤♣

The End Is In Sight

So Why Put Up A Fight

Every Man Will Say

Every Dog Has Its' Day

Comin' To Terms

With Whatever U've Learned

Was Jus' To Prepare You

For The Way

Don't Wait For Me

Cos I'm Jus' Breakin' Free

An' Everyone Mus' Fulfil

Their Own Destiny

Not Jus' Because

You Did It For Love

Or Jus' To Gain' A Place

In The Kingdom Above

The Harder You Try

Still U're Dissatisfied

Now There's No Relief

From The Pressures On U're Mind

Careful What You Wish For

B'Cos You Might Receive

All Of The Things

You Like To Believe

Here's A Little Somethin'

To Set Aside

For The Offerin'

Of The Alms' An' The Tithes'

Somethin' To Consider

In Spite Of U'reself

Maybe You Didn't Think

To Help Somebody Else. ☆

NIGHTMARE

There Are Some I Would Contend
That Simply Want This World To End

Without Nothing Left To Exploit Again
Except A War Of Their Consequence

There Are Those I Would Suppose
Are Nothing More Than Enemies An' Foes

In Being Friendly When It Seems
Their Real Ambitions Are Often Unseen

There Are Those I Understand
That Hold Us All To This Ransom

Though Its' Hard To Prove Their Nefarious Plans
We Must Be Prepared To Take Our Stand

There Are Those Who Control
All The Resources Of This Globe

An' Yet We All Must Pay Heed
Before This Nightmare Kills Our Dreams. ☆

SLEDGEHAMMER

♣♠♣

You Waited Until

We Were Deeply In Love

Before You Pull The Plug

Before You Had Enough

You Waited Until

We Stood On Solid Ground

Before You Pull The Rug

Before You Fit Me Up

You Waited Until

I Took Another Pill

An' Then After The Thrill

A Changin' Reality

You Set Me Up

To Hook Me On That Stuff

Now I'm Addicted It Seems

I'm At Another Extreme

You Played A Part

In Sabotagin' My Heart

You Did A Number On Me

Forgettin' What I Could Be

From The Rise An' Fall

I Could Have Had It All

But Now Its' Nothin' To Me

Nuthin' But Real Poetry

For All Of The Hopes

That I Ever Had

Makin' Me Glad

You Wasn't Happy For Me

An' Now The Sledgehammer

Is In U're Hands

An' Now U're Smashin' My Plans

Destroyin' All Of My Dreams. ☆

SUMMER

♣♤♧

Since I Got U're Telegram
I See U've All Bein' Makin' Plans

Instantly U've Bein' Transformin'
From That All That CO2, From All That Global Warmin'

Now My Part Time Friends Come Wanderin' In
Defrostin' From Those Winter Winds

I Guess Its' Jus' Another Thermal Explosion
Its' Jus' Another Cold Frost Freezin' Up The Ocean

An' All Of The Love That's Being Displayed
You Can't Seem To Find Jus' To Give It Away

An' Life Has Become Like A Movie Scene
But That Movie Scene Ain't Movin' Me

An' All Of The Money, That You Made
Paradin' Aroun' On That New World Stage

As All The Groovy Newbie's Are Frontin' Their Fashion
The Economy's Crashin', The Stocks Are Comin' Down

An' All Of Things That Were Left Try To Create
Plastered On A Landscape Of Digital Hate

I Guess The Abstract Things Are Jus' Normal Now
Well Its' A Formal Thing To Stand Out In A Crowd

Now It Seems That Time Is A Commodity
As Were Tryin' To Break Free This Entity

The Processes Of A Mother Nature
The Pro-Creator, Is Jus' Another Machine

It Seems Were Only Good For The Summer
Despite All The Rain An' All Of The Thunder

Another Year Without Closure
A Sudden Downpour, Then Its' All Over. ☆

I MUS' BE PREPARED
(AT ANY TIME TO CARRY ON)

♣♤♣

I Seen Him Walkin' By

With The Girl Of My Dreams

I Seen The Hollywood Lights

Create Every Scene

I Seen The Statue Of Liberty

Standin' So Tall

Still I Mus' Be Prepared

At Any Time To Carry On

I Seen The Desert In Nevada

Area 1 0 1

I Seen An' Undergroun' Bunker

For When They Drop The Bomb

I Seen Them Tryin' To Climb

Over That Mexico Wall

Still I Mus' Be Prepared

At Any Time To Carry On

Could Be An' Earthquake Eruptin'

In The San Andreas Fault

Or Tryin' To Catch A Cable Car

In San Francisco

Standin' In Grand Central

Waitin' For You To Show

Still I Mus' Be Prepared

At Any Time To Carry On. ☆

3. त्रयः.ሶስት

POETICALDICTION

जब्रिबा.የጽባ जब्बा.ጀባ पक्षी.ወፍ

THE ONE

Its' The Face, That Launched A Thousand Ships
Its' A Red Rose Thorn Upon U're Fingertips

Its' The Sweetest Taste Upon U're Bitter Lips
Its' The Time You Thought This Must Be It

An' So Now You, As You Face The Day
In Sight Of The Ones, Who Would Turn You Away

So You Turn, To Hope In Bitter Faith
But Its' The Longest Road That You Have To Take

Would It Be Betta' If It Was Just A Lie
That Someone You Love Could Only Make You Cry

The One That You Longed For Every Night
The One You Bein' Searchin' For All Of U're Life For

So You Welcome All Of U're Pain
You Believe You Deserve, U're Not The One To Blame

But There's Nothing Left For You To Gain
To Wallow In Self-Pity, To Escape All The Shame

Its' Always The One Who Got Away
Its' Always The One, Who Would Make You Stay

Its' Always The One You Would Love Forever
Its' Always The One But You Would Never Say Never. ☆

ALL IN HIS NAME

♣♠♣

The Closer We Get

The Further We Are

From All Of The Things

That Truly Matter

From The Start Of This Life

An' All That We Lead

Is Nothin' To Compare

To Eternity

In The Absence Of Truth

Its' Jus' Wishful Thinkin'

Cos There's No Other Way

To Stop This Ship From Sinkin'

Despite What You Think

This Ship Is Goin' Down

Its' Either Sink Or Swim

Before You Finally Drown

Its' Time To Decide

If U're Deeply Affected

We All Know What Its' Like

To Be Cheated An' Rejected

Still Tryin' To Get Back

To What It Use To Be

But Ask U'reself One Question

What Do You Believe

No Matta' The Game

You Happen To Play

If We Can't Even Change It

Then Its' All In Vain

You Can Do It The Wrong

Or The Righteous Way

If We Dare To Proclaim It

All In His Name. ☆

THE WOMBMAN
(MOTHER OF ALL THINGS)

♣♠♣

Forever We Search Through All Of Her Virtues
The Innocence Spent In The Days Of Her Youth

Revered By The Essence In All Of Her Presence
A Desecrated Violet Upon A Pedestal

An' So They Sold An' Bought You, For Slavery's Fortune
A Handsome Wage An Unfortunate Girl

But What Replaces This Hate Were Left To Celebrate
As She Could Only Escape Inside Of Herself

Since The Maternal Provenance In A Garden Of Promises
She Cultivates Her Little Eden An' Calls It Home

So Afraid To Believe In, From The Fear Of Bein' Deceived
A Legendary Tale That Never Grows Old

An' What Appears To Be Is The Mother Of All Things
As She Follows The Evenin' In The Afternoon

Still The Wombman Is A Mystery
Much Before History Was Told. ☆

THE MUTHA'

♣♠♣

Hustlin' On The Job

Daddy Couldn't Afford It

Robbin' Peter To Pay Paul

Anotha' Ghetto Story

Livin' Like Its' Large

On That Welfare Check

That Used Up Credit Card

With The Bailiffs Breathin'

Down Ya' Neck

Yes I've Seen Those Lovers

Lyin' On A Bed Of Roses

Actin' Like Their Kings N' Queens

Tryin' To Keep Up With Joneses

It Seems We Bought The Dream

But We Simply Can't Afford It

An' So We Pay The Price

The Sacrifice Of A Ghetto Story

We Had Such Big Ideas

Well Holy Roller Its' Moses

Sundays After Church

Some Black Eyed Peas

An' Good Cookin'

I Guess I'm Reminiscin'

About The Things That We Had

Some Ghetto Memories

Always Seem To Take You Back

But Who, Who Turn The Mutha' Out

Was It You, Who Turn The Mutha' Out

A Struggle To Survive

To Keep The Family Alive

But Who, Who Turn The Mutha' Out. ☆

SAVED

♣♤♣

All U're Best Made Plans
    Are Laid To Waste
        As U're Waitin' On
            That Sabbath Day

An' All U're Messages
    Brought The Messenger Down
        I See U've Made U're Mark
            On This Hallowed Ground

I'm Takin' This From The Premise
    That You Already Know
        So I Don't Need To Remind You
            Of What's Gone Before

I Won't Try To Assert
    Or Preach It To The Converted
        I Think U've Suffered Enough
            I Think There's Too Much Hurtin'

Of All The Things That You Said
    Brought Me To My Knees
        But Can The End
            Justify All Of The Means

For All Of The Things
    That Have Come Before
        No Matter How Far I Stray
            I Always Knock At The Door

Now There's Symbols An' Signs
    For Every Chapter An' Verse
        Now There's Prophets An' Poets
        Recitin' These Words

Now There's Somethin' For Nothin'
    For The Life That He Gave
        An' All U're Love Was Saved. ☆

WHITE DOVE
♧♤♧

The Flesh Is Tired

An' The Body Is Weak

The Spirit Is Willin'

To Conquer Defeat

U're Eyes Are Failin'

But Hopin' To See

A Sweet Surrender

A Peaceful Victory

I'm Listenin'

To The Voices Of Karma

Discernin' Much Wisdom

As They Speak

The Cosmic Words

Of U're Future

The Transmigration

Of U're Destiny

The Rumours Of War

Echoes Like A Trumpet

Usherin' In

The Sounds Of Peace

A Breath Of Freedom

Might Bring You Some Comfort

Until All Bondage

Is Finally Released

So Whisper A Prayer

Of Supplications

Send Me A White Dove

Of U're Mercy

Contemplate With Me

A Quiet Meditation

Show Me The Offerins'

Of An' Olive Branch Tree. ☆

THE RIGHT STUFF

Life Is Like A Crazy Maze
I Guess Were Always Tryin' To Work It Out
Forgettin' The Days Becomes A Matta' Of Years
An' Time Is Always Runnin' Out

Life Is Full Of Make-Believe
Where Dreams An' Fantasies Are Pursued
An' Yet We All Want Somethin' Real
That Validates Our Curiosity

Life Is Like A Circle In A Square
Still We Try To Defy All The Angles
An' Yet There's Nuthin' To Compare
Even When All The Questions
Have All Bein' Answered

The World Could Be A Betta' Place
If Only We All Knew The Right Stuff
Still You Can't Preten' To Find Happiness
Somethin' Like True Love
You Jus' Can't Make It Up. ☆

LIFE AFTER DEATH

♣♠♣

Why Is Mankind

So Fascinated With Space

When All We See Aroun' Us

Are Only Crimes Against Humanity

Our Faith We May Have Misplaced

Runnin' Towards Those Days Of Reckonin'

The Days That Were Countin' Down

Sealin' Our Fate With Such Cruelty

If Lies Could Not Undo

What We Call The Truth

Is Our Revelation

If Time Is Not The End

Then Why Do Choose To Live In Illusions

Is There Life After Death

When There's Nothin' Left

For Us To Destroy

Will There Be A Second Chance

Anotha' Birth To Replenish The Earth. ☆

HOPE AN' PRAY

The Left Of The Right, The Right Of The Wrong

The Centre Of Nowhere, Where Do We Belong

Nuthin' To Believe, Believe Anythin'

Love Is U're Family, U're Next Of Kin

The Good An' The Bad, The Lies Are All True

Nobody's Listenin', But They're Talkin' To You

U're Faith In The Future, Is All In The Past

Nuthin' From Nuthin', Is Guaranteed To Last

The End Of The World, Is Waitin' To Be Saved

Before You Get In, Please Get Out Of The Way

The Days Are Numbered, Its' A Matta' Of Time

Before You Lose What You Lost

I Hope You Find Peace Of Mind

Whatever We Can't Do Without

Whatever We Need To Make A Breakthrough

I Hope That We Can Work It Out

I Hope An' Pray That We Can See It Through. ☆

THINGS THAT GO WITH THINGS

(A PUZZLE)

♣♠♣

There Are Some Wants

There Are Some Needs

There Are Some Destinies

Forever Unravellin'

There Are Some Days

That Simply Blur An' Fade

There Are Some Days

That Quickly Come An' Go

There Are Memories,

Like Rivers An' Streams

There Are Things To Remember

An' Things To Let Go

Sometimes You See

What You Choose To Believe

But There's Only One Thing

Inside Of U're Soul

There Are Some Things

That Go With Something

An' Yet There Are Things

We Still Don't Know

There Are Some Things

That Never Seem To Fit

Pieces Of A Dream

Jus' Like A Puzzle. ☆

CHORUS OF ANGELS

Seven Past Ten
Its' Way Past Heaven
Seven Thousand Years
Ten Hundred Mo' We Bein' Waitin'
Seraphim's An' Cherubim's
Sing Besides The Altar
The Whispering Of Silent Hymns
Fills The Air With Prayers
I Guess You An' I Had A Deal
I Guess That Seal Is What I'm Askin' For
Even Though I Don't Know What It Reveals
Well I Guess Its' Jus' A Question
Waitin' To Be Answered
I Was Told Long Ago
But Now I'm Old I've Forgotten
You Can Walk An' Rest A While
Even Though We Ain't Stoppin'
We Can Tell That A Fairytale
Is Like A Spell That Were Weavin'
Like A Sermon On Top Of A Hill
We Find It Hard To Believe In
Yes I Know I Can't Pretend
I Know Its' Only Beginning
But The Ending Of This Song
Begins With A Chorus Of Angels. ☆

PILGRIM

♣♠♣

The Broken An' Lame

Are Beggin' On The Streets

As The Scornful Mockers

Conceal Their Deceit

So You Offer Them Water

An' Somethin' To Eat

As This Pilgrim Is Humbled,

By Washin' Their Feet

Fallin' In Love

With Solomon's Song

Shulamites' An' Virgins

Can Do You No Wrong

So U've Come To The Palace

Of Many A' Room

With The Incense An' Chalice

Fit For A Pilgrims Tomb

Goin' In Search

Of The Holy Grail

Uncoverin' The Shroud

Where The Body Was Laid

A Strangers Pilgrim

In A Foreign Land

A Sign Of The Times

Sinkin' In Quicksand

Many Are Called

But Few Are Chosen

An' He That Feels It

Surely Knows It

It Comes With A Price

Of Which Their Demandin'

But No Man Can Lean

On His Own Understandin'. ☆

ENERGY SERENITY

You Know U're Jus' Dead Meat
On These Beat Up Streets
That's When God Sent The Devil
Jus' To Cum Get Me

A Fatalistic Life
Cuts You Like A Knife
While Paradise Is Sleepin'
On The Floor Outside

Sum' People Live In The Dark
Of The Amusement Park
I Guess The Times Are Rough'
I Guess The Times Are Hard

Still They're Diggin' Their Graves
Now That The Dues Are Paid
An' They'll Be Makin' Their Claims
By The Old Arcade

Its' Jus' Another Death Wish
Wishin' I Could Live
Forever In This Love
Forever In This Myth

So Who U're Tryin' To Be
I Hope U're Not Like Me
Another Organ Grinder
With Another Monkey

Why Don't You Show Me Sum' Luv'
C'mon An' Hit Me Up
An' We Can Ride The Waves
Of This Energy

Why Don't You Show Me Sum' Luv'
An' All The Other Stuff
An' We Can Ride This Groove
Like Serenity. ☆

ONE-SIDED DREAM
(STEADY UP MY HEART)
♣♤♣

So What Can You Do

With U're Ego Shot Thru'

I Guess Me An' You

Had A Secret Deal

But Who Can You Trust

When U've Run Out Of Luck

Well I've Always Held Up

My Part Of This Bargain

I Tried To Keep To The Straights

But It Might Be Too Late

They're Always Changin' Lanes

Ziggin' An' Zaggin'

I Thought About Breakin' Free

Bendin' Down On My Knees

If There's A Prayer Left For Me

Somethin' To Believe In

Sometimes Its' Hard To Explain

That U're Goin' Insane

As They Come Closer To Cut

U're Jugular Vein

I Thought That They Understood

But Understandin's No Good

They'd Rather Take It All

An' Bury You In A Grave

An' Now My Eyes Can See

In This Reality

Well Its' A Lonely Affair

A One-Sided Dream

But Right From The Start

I Guess I Played My Part

Now Its' Gonna Take Some Love

To Steady Up My Heart. ☆

THE CROOKED PATH

People Are Fightin' For A Right
A Human Right You Thought Was Never U'res

In Spite Of The Light, Shinin' Bright
Has Left You Confounded Walkin' In The Dark

You Can Lead A Horse To Water
But I Can't Tell You What To Think

About This Knowledge Goin' Aroun'
Coz Now Its' Goin' Down The Sink

When You Go Lookin For A Friend
That's When You Find There's No One Around

As There Too Busy Diggin' Ditches
Tryin' To Bury The Rest Of Humankind

An' The Churches Doors Are Always Open
To Feed The Hungry An' Poor

An' Those Of Us Who Were Forgotten
In The Battle For The Common Law

So We Try To Run This Human Race
With So Little Time Left To Walk

So You Always Think That U're Gonna Win
You Never Believe You Can Lose It All

Before You Lay U're Burdens On The Heap
An' Wonder What The Cross Is For

As You Try To Fly An' Navigate The Sky
An' Wonder Why The Stars Never Fall

Now The Time Has Come To Pull U're Own Weight
No Matter How You Zig-Zag It Aroun'

Now There's No More Lanes To Lay It Straight
Coz We Always End Up On The Crooked Path. ☆

AN' OLD FASHIONED WAY

We're Always Takin' Turns

Still The Young Never Learn

Jus' How This Candle Burns

At Both Ends

Some Will Look In A Glance

Takin' You By The Hand

Leadin' You By Chance

We Begin To Sway

Maybe You Had The Best

So Why Settle For Less

Since The Days Of Romance

Are Beginnin' To Fade

An' As We Move Out Of Step

Maybe The Music Slept

Thru' The Tears As We Sang

Those Old Melodies

Like An' Innocent Kiss

Can Make You Reminisce

Like When We Use To Dance

In An' Old Fashioned Way. ☆

FRUIT OF U'RE SIN

♧♤♧

You Wanted It All, But You Jus' Couldn't Handle
A Piece Of The Pie, By Takin' A Sample
An' So You Forget, What You Already Had
This Is U're Story, An' The Story's So Sad

Remember They Told You, There's No Place Like Home
But U've Bein' Wanderin' Far, An' Wanderin' Long
A Prodigal Son Who's Made His Mistakes
Wonderin' Now If The Future Still Waits

An' So History Repeats Once Again
But Only A Fool Would Do What U're Doin'
I Guess You Think Its' A Game, Or A Comical Thing
But When It All Falls Apart, Nobody's Laughin'

Serious Is As Serious Does
But Nobody's Jokin' About Fallin' In Love
But Ain't It Strange, Seasons Can Change
But There's Only 4 Seasons, There's Only 4 Names

Only You Know What U've Done
The Story Continues An' Jus' Goes On
An' So You Begin To Shed U're Skin
A Serpent In The Garden, An' The Fruit Of U're Sin. ☆

THE LATE AFTERNOON
♧♤♧

It Was A Dictatorial Catalyst

For A Puritan Theocracy

Where The Credit Card Capitalist

With Their Dispersed Assets

Await The New Frontier

Of The Sonic Boom

As The Domesticated Mercenaries

We're Pleadin' Their Poverty

Outside The Local Commune

An' Yet The Possibility's Zero

For All The War Heroes

Still Waitin' For Godot

In The Late Afternoon. ☆

PROVE A POINT

You Said I Seem To Go A Long Way
To Prove A Point
When I Don't Understand
If There's A Point To Be Made
Its' Kinda Hard To Know
Where U're Coming From
If I Don't Know You
I Don't Know Anyone
No Matter How I Fall
It Ends In Disarray
As If My Choices In Love
Would Always End Up This Way
As I Came Face To Face
With All The Powers That Be
Within Those Darkest Hours
The Powers Inside Of Me
You Said I Seem To Go A Long Way
To Prove A Point
Well I Don't Understand
If There's A Point To Be Made
Its' Kinda Hard To Know
Where U're Coming From
If I Don't Know You
I Don't Know Anyone. ☆

FIX THE ROOF
♣♤♣

I've Bein' Down Every Avenue

Tryin' To Raise Myself Some Revenue

Jus' To Take Care, The Likes Of You

In The Here An' The Now

I Guess The Present Won't Do

God Only Knows

About Those Slings An' Arrows

But On This Hallowed Groun'

This 33 Ain't Shallow

So What's Between You An' Me

If You Lead Then I'll Follow

Let's Consecrate It Today

Why Leave It Til' Tomorrow

As Much As We're Prepared

To Make This Small Proviso'

Generations Will Come

Seekin' Out Their Sanctum

Whatever You May Need

Could Mean U're Soul Survival

Upto Until The Last

An' The First On Arrival

I Guess Its' High Time To Fix The Roof

Now That The Sun Is Shinin'

So Plant U're Garden In The East

So That U're Eyes Can See

We Finished What We Started. ☆

MURPHY'S LAW

♧♤♧

They Say That Stars Often Collide
Jus' Like People, Me An' You
Sometimes It Turns Out To Be Bad
Sometimes It Turns Out To Be Good

As Much As We Try To Empathize
Takin' Someone's Place, In Someone Else's Shoes
No Matta' How We Try To Get It Right
There's Always Somethin' Frustratin'
That We Can Never Do

It Seems Our Mistakes Are Out In The Open
Only Breakin' What's Broken
Its' Never Kind To Be Cruel
It Seems That The Signs On A Billboard Poster
Are Even Harda' To Follow
When You Don't Know The Rules

I Thought You Knew Me, But You Don't
Thought You Would Understand
But I Know That You Won't
An' All This Pain That We Carry Inside
Well Its' No Wonda' What We Hide Behind

As We Try To Change Our Circumstances
How Could Somethin' So Right End Up So Wrong
An' What Seems To Take You By Surprise
All Comes Down To Murphy's Law. ☆

FAIR

♣♠♣

When I Was With Her

When You Was With Him

I Wanted You Mo'

Mo' Than I Could Imagine

An' It Fills Me With Dread

Coz U're Inside Of My Head

An' Its' The Reason I Know

Why My Soul Is Why Misled

If Love Is A Sin

When Did It Really Begin

An' When Did This Pastime

Become A Casual Thing

Like A Fish From The Side

The Taste Of Sweet Apple Pie

We're A Match Made In Heaven

No One Can Deny

I Guess Its' A Mess

Jus' Like A Pregnancy Test

If Only We Met Before

We Slept With Somebody Else

But How Could We Know

When It Was Long Ago

An' Now This Life That We Lead

Has Left Us Yearin' For Mo'

In This Garden We Find

Love Is So Blind

Coz An' When I'm Lookin' At You

I See God In U're Eyes

Its' Jus' A Love Affair

Where Nobody Cares

Now That We Found Out

Its' Jus' Too Late To Be Fair. ☆

THE CITY SPIRIT

The Sun Lights The Moon All Aglow
An' There's Something Else
I Thought You Should Know
Well I Guess I Never Told You So
But I'm Going To A Place
Where I Can't Find Myself

Before This Moment Starts To Fade
Today Is Only Tomorrows Yesterday
When There's Nothing Else That I Can Say
But I'm Going To A Place
Where I Can't Find Myself

I Wasn't Looking For A Star
But I Lost My Shadow
Somewhere In The Dark
An' Before We Had This Heart To Heart
I Was Going To A Place
Where I Can't Find Myself

I Guess I Made The Same Mistakes
An' Then Repeat The Same Whole Thing Again
Running Away To Escape My Fate
I'm Going To A Place
Where I Can't Find Myself

It Seems That Pain Is Here To Stay
An' Somehow The Hurt It Never Goes Away
A Disappointment You Might Say
But I'm Going To A Place
Where I Can't Find Myself

I Always Meet You In The End
We Always Return An' Go Back There Again
Even Though U're My Best Friend
I'm Going To A Place
Where I Can't Find Myself

The City Spirit Upon These Streets
Always Sings A Song That Sounds So Sweet
Its' About These Strangers Who Never Meet
Except For Their Eyes Out Of Curiosity. ☆

WRECKERS OF LIFE
(RABBIT HOLE)

U've Lost An' U've Gambled

An' U've Gambled Again

Still Believin' Somehow

U're Gonna Win In The End

As The Trials Of Denial

An' The Truth You Defend

Has Cost You All Of U're Money

An' All Of U're Friends

You Can Take All Of Ya' Chances

But You Might Pay The Price

Thinkin' All Of The Wrong Things

That Won't See You Right

You Can Turn Off The Lights

Before You Go To Bed

To Keep Away All Of The Demons

Inside Of U're Head

I See You Climbin' The Walls

While Tryin' Not To Fall

I See U're Lost In The Halls

An' All The Corridors

I've Seen The Revolvin' Doors

Goin' Roun' An' Roun'

As You Go Walkin' In

Tryin' To Find U're Way Out

Well Its' A Roll Of The Dice

For The Wreckers Of Life

Stranded An' Abandoned

By The Grief An' The Strife

I Watch It All Disappear

As You Surrender U're Soul

I Watch You Disappear

Into That Rabbit Hole. ☆

LOVE IS ALIVE

For All Of The Dreams You Were Sold
You Never Believed You Could Be Compromised
For All Of The Times, You Wore That Cross
Escapin' This Fate To Be Crucified

As Much As We've All Bein' Exposed
Shot Through The Apparel, All Riddled With Holes
Praying Every Day An' Every Night
Waitin' On Faith, For U're Soul To Be Saved

Whatever It Takes To Reach A State Of Grace
Whatever We've Done Wrong
We Know Its' Taken Too Long
Hoping For That Heaven In Time An' Space
A Kind Of Surrender, A Different Kind Of Place

Maybe U're Messiah Is Already Here
Or The Substitution Of Another Lie
Maybe U're Saviour Has Already Come
An' U're The Living Proof That Love Is Alive. ☆

FALSE START
♣♠♣

After The Pain

What Do You Gain

People Often Change

Into Someone Else

After You Bleed

What Do You Need

A Self-Help Book

A New Philosophy

After You Know

Where Can You Go

Talkin' To U'reself

An' Walkin' Alone

After U've Said

What's Inside Of U're Head

You Somehow Got The Feelin'

You Being Were Misled

She's Talkin' Me Out Of Love

She's Turnin' Me Down

She's Pushin' Me Out The Door

She Doesn't Need Me Aroun'

Funny How The Light

Always Plays With U're Senses

Now U're In State

Of Heightened Awareness

Somethin' That You Share

With U're Contemporaries

An' Elation Of The Heart

Or Jus' Anotha' False Start. ☆

EGO

♧♤♧

You Say You Want Nothing, Nothing At All
But All That You Ask, Is For Everything An' Mo'

You Think Its' Alright To Change U're View
As Long As You Have The Right To Pick An' Choose

U're Full Of Big Ideas, But You Don't Know What It Is
U're Full Of Inspiration, In U're Gut Instincts

U're So Privately Curious Behind Closed
But The Privacy You Seek Has Left You Yearnin' For Mo'

Of All The Wander, Of All Of The Lust
Its' No Wonder Why You Have No One To Trust

To Be Free As A Bird An' Like A Honey Bee
But This Freedom U've Taken Too Seriously

An' They Can't Free You From That Gilded Cage
An' The Sycophants That You Entertain

From The Obscenities Of A Mortal Sin
Is When U're Ego Begins To Shed Its' Skin. ☆

IF ONLY

♧♤♧

The Depiction Of A Picture

Could Be The Whisper Of A Scripture

Pour The Elixir For A Mixture

A Faithful Religion For A Believer

In The Doorways An' Alleyways

Of The Cities An' Streets

In The Urban Suburban

Of The Towns An' Villages

The Common Enemy

Of The Common Good

In The Absence Of God

Where Is U're Love

For The Eyes, The Ears

The Hearts An' The Minds

For The Words Of A Vision

Sustained An' Revived

For All That Was Said

Would You Come Back To Find

All That We Fear

In Being Left Behind

If Only You Heeded

What Was Defeated

If Only You'd Spoken

To All That Was Broken

If Only You Accepted

What Was Rejected

If Only You'd Restore

A Spirit Like Before. ☆

RUN N' HIDE

Standing By The Side Of A Grave
The One That's Marked With U're Birth Name

Its' A Stone Cold Feelin' Of Somethin' So Strange
That You Should Be Aware Of What Heaven Says

Somewhere Behind The Gates Of Hell
Is A Soul That Cries Locked Inside A Cage

Its' An' Endless Dream From Which You Never Wake
That You Should Be Afraid Of What Heaven Says

The Gravity Of All Eternity
Is Jus' The Weight Of The World Restin' On You An' Me

An' All Humanity Wants Their Freedom Today
But You Should Be Aware Of What Heaven Says

Its' A Long, Long Time To Bare With This Life
Somewhere Out On The Edge Tryin' To Survive

An' The Fear Of God, Is Enough In U're Mind
To Make A True Believer Try To Run An' Hide. ☆

WE WERE KIDS
♣♤♣

You Always Wanna Take Me
  Down Memory Lane
    Sayin' Things Were Really Betta'
    Back In Those Days

But The Past I Remember
  Wasn't Always Like This
    An' Not So Good
      As You Like To Think It Is

  I Know You Always Wish
    You Could Go Back Again
      If Jus' To Relive
        U're Greatest Memories

In That Innocent Place
  Where Our Dreams
    Once Were Made
      When You An' I Use To Play
        In That Sun Shiny Haze

I Understand We Were Younger
  In Those Early Days
    I Understand The Emotions
      An' Dreams Were Made

I Know The Reasons Why
    You Might Think Like That
        If Only To Find
            The Feelins' We Once Had

I Know You Liken' The Past
    Unto A Paradise
        A Perfect Place In Time
            Of Eternal Sunshine

Don't Wanna Burst U're Bubble
    Or Destroy That Myth
        But That's How It Was
            When We Were Kids. ☆

NUTHIN' MO'

♣♤♣

I Fear I've Become

The Child I Could Not Save

Runnin' Towards The Future

An' Swallowed Up By An' Empty Grave

Oblivious To The Fortunes

Of Why My Bed Was Made

Watchin' For A Distant Star

The Only One That Never Stayed

A Mental State Of Slavery

Now Begins To Take Its' Toll

As Of Yet There's No Remedy

For The Young Or Even The Old

If Only I Could Resist

To Avoid This Doom An' Gloom

If Only I Could Return

An' Find My Way

Back Into The Womb

I Fear That I've Become

The Old Man That I Despised

While Cursin' My Own Misfortunes

An' Strugglin' With One Day At A Time

Once They Push You Over The Edge

Now They're Tellin' You How To Live

Until U're Spirit Begins To Break

An' You Got Nuthin'

Nuthin' Left To Give

Why Did We Even Come Here

If There's Nuthin' Mo'

Nuthin' Mo' Than This

Whatever We Were Hopin' To Find

I Think That We've Already

We've Already Missed. ☆

LONELY TOWN

After The Rush Has Turned Into A Crawl
There's No One Here, Jus' Me On My Own

After The Climb, Turns Into A Fall
There's No One Here, There's No One At All

The Final Curtain, Is Almost Certain
After The Hurtin' Has Come An' Gone

An' All You Contain Jus' To Numb All The Pain
Is A Solitary Feelin' Of A Beatin' Heart

So Where Can You Go, When The Feelin' Is Low
When The Window Is Closed An' The Door Is Locked

Somewhere Inside These Four Walls
You Lose What You Had, You Forget What You Got

An' There's No One Left To Let Me Down
An' There's No More Places To Hang Around

An' There's Nothing Left For Me Now
Besides Myself In This Lonely Town. ☆

POWER

♣♤♧

Some People Say U're Legit
Some People Say That U're Regal

Some People Say That U'll Never Pass
Through The Eye Of A Needle

I Guess You Like The Dynamics
Of Keepin' Us In This Status Quo

All The While Keepin' Up Appearances
As You Maintain The Perfect Role

You Mus' Be Somebody Untouchable
A Social Pedigree Of U're Own

As You Seem To Be Completely Immune
An' Safely Protected By The Arms Of The Law

You Hide Behind Double Standards
Without Even Droppin' A Clue

Somewhere Inside U're Ivory Tower
Nuthin' Seems To Spoil U're Perfect View

I Suppose The Rules Of Engagement
Simply Don't Apply To You

You Seem To Have All The Advantage
You Seem To Have All The Power Too. ☆

JESUS
(THEN SHALL THE END COME)

♣♠♣

Today Of All Days

To Abate My Fears

Yeh' Tonight Is The Night

I Need A Remedy

I Hope My Ship Comes In

Steadily An' Readily

As U're Forefathers

An' U're Foremothers

An' U're Forebrothers

An' U're Foresisters

An' The Descendants

Of U're Abraham

Have Been Scattered Across

This Holy Land

Tonight Is The Night

The Light Dimly Shines

With The Weight Of The World

Now On My Mind

Yeh' Tonight Is The Night

An' The Tables Have Turned

An' Today Is The Day

That I Begin To Learn

Of Who To Uphold

An' Who To Denounce

As You Come To Put Me Out

The House Of My Espouse

From All The Petitions

That They Made Before

As They Keep On Fightin'

These Tribal Wars

Tonight Is The Night

For An' Achin' Heart

An' Those Vacancies

In The Arms Of Love

Yeh' Tonight Is The Night

When We Come To Depart

To Take Some Comfort

In The Ragin' Storm

Jus' Like The Sermon

Upon The Mount

Before All This Truth

Comes Tumblin' Down

From The Root Of David

An' The Stem Of Jesse

Pittin' One Against The Otha'

As The World Is Re-Set

Jesus Is Real

No Matta'

What You Feel. ☆

SOLITUDE

♧♤♧

The Sharpest Words, Are Superficial
Upon The Membrane, A Striking Blow
The Haunting Reminder Of Paranoia
The Scars Are Deep, The Cuts Are Shallow
An' Unrepentant Lamentation
The Injustices Of Which To Boast
The Crimes Committed For Salvation
A Poor Man's Religion, In An' Unjust World
A Confidence Trick Of Habitual Habits
The Constant Addiction Of A Sickly Need
An' Earthly Desire Of Flesh To Unravel
An' Eye To Behold, A Love ILL-Conceived
A God To Defy, A Devil Denied
Hiding By Day An' Seeking By Night
A Lawless Nature Of Constrained Misdeeds
The Plight Of A Nightmare The Releasing Of Dreams
The Death An' The Dying, The Dead An' Deceased
One Breath At A Time, Until There's Nothing To Breathe
Moriah, Golgotha An' Calvary
Where The Arc Of The Sky, Meets The Land An' The Sea
A Tourniquet Will Stop The Bleeding
A Rub Of Salt Into The Wound
A Pack Of Ice For The Bruises
A Fortress Heart In Solitude. ☆

MIRACLE

♣♠♣

I Guess They Never
    Understood The Song
        Or The Reasons Why
            We Always Get It Wrong

        Why You Wanna Put U'reself
          Through So Much Pain
          Time After Time
            Again An' Again

So How Many Hearts
    Does It Really Take
        For Us To Stop Repeating
        The Same Mistakes

        No Matter How Strange
          U're Sweet Refrain
          The Sadistic Truths
            Will Always Remain

Somehow We Believe
   In This Fairytale
      Has Gotta' Be Reasons
         Why We Must Prevail

         As Sure As U're Heart
           Could Never Ever Fail
             Still The Same Ole' Song
               Goes On For Always

No Matter How Nice
   We Find The Melody
      Its' The Same Ole'
         Songs Of Tragedy

         Lovers Try To Find It
         But Rarely Do
           Coz It Takes Nothing
             Short Of A Miracle. ☆

SOMETHING DIFFERENT
♣♠♣

Wastin' Time, Waitin' In Line

Hopin' For Something Better

Remember The Game

Well It Never Changed

An' Now Its' Time

For Somethin' Different

Funny How Friends

Become Somethin' Else

Under The Spotlight

Of Famous People

Before You Left Town

I Saw You Turn It Around

An' Now Its' Time

For Somethin' Different

An' Where Are You Now

Shadows An' Clouds

I Wish You'd Return

From U're Exile

Just To Begin

A New An' Beautiful Thing

Coz Now Its' Time

For Somethin' Different

It Was You That Said

We Could Do It Again

But The First Time

Was Always Much Better

An' Now I See

What Magic Could Be

Now That Its' Time

For Somethin' Different. ☆

CARNIVAL

♣♠♣

Say That Life Is A Celebration
An' Invitation We've All Bein' Waitin' For

Say That Love Has Affected You
Well U're Welcome To The Carnival

Say That Stars Are The Laws Of Attraction
The Processions Begun But Where Are You

Say That Words Meet With U're Satisfaction
Well U're Welcome To The Carnival

Say That Venus An' Mars Needs No Introductions
I'm Frozen To The Bone Until I'm Touchin' You

Say We Stand Alone With No Interruptions
Until We Bare Our Souls At The Carnival

Say True Love Is A Beautiful Feelin'
There's No Reasons Why We Feel Like We Do

Say Were Wide Awake While Were Still Dreamin'
I'm Dreamin' Of You At The Carnival

Its' In U're Eyes But I Don't Know What I Feel
If I Can Say It But I Can't Make It Real

If I Were Certain, If I Was True
We Could Celebrate It At The Carnival. ☆

9 MONTHS OR MORE
♣♠♣

Now That We've Reached

The Very End

It Seems We Weren't

Really Friends At All

An' So For Now We Can Drop

The Pretence

All The Fun An' Games

What Was It For

Right At The Very

Same Point In Time

I'm Thinking How

Could It Happen To Me Twice

Instead Killing

2 Birds With One Stone

I'm Taken By Surprise

Its' Just A Pack Of The Lies

An' If We Ever

Get Out Of Here

I Guess U'll Be With Him

An' Watch Me Disappear

As U're Words

Come Falling To Distort

I Guess Its' All Bein' Paid

I Guess Its' Already Bought

Coz When I Hear

Those Golden Notes

There's Only 4 Seasons

Inside Of Our Souls

Remindin' Me

Of September Again

Comin' Around

In 9 Months Or More. ☆

END OF A TALE

There Was A Bookstop By The Door
It Kept It Ajar So It Wouldn't Close

Til The Curious Child Picked It Up An' Looked In
Closing The Door, That Locked Him In

The Silence Was Violent Inside Of His Mind
Sifting Through Words Of Ladders To Climb

A Voice Cried Out But He Didn't Respond
He Jus' Kept On Readin' Of Places Beyond

The Sound Of A Knockin' On The Door
But He Kept On Readin', Tryin' To Ignore

Jus' One More Word Before They Broke In An' Saw
Removin' The Book, To Put It Back As It Was

Nine Inch Nails An' All The Details
The Devils Instruments Began To Prevail

The Stories A Journey, His Mind Set A Sail
To Get To The End Of A Tale. ☆

ASCENDIN'

♣♠♣

Life It Always Changes

Its' Always Rearranges

Under The Influence

Of The Moon An' The Sun

Its' Written In The Stars

If Don't Know Who You Are

Its' Takin' Root An' Shape

On The Groun'

Faith Is The Key

To U're Destiny

Even Though Its' Not The End

Of The Story

The Things We Believe

Are Full Of Mysteries

Its' Jus' The Past An' The Present

An' The Future Repeatin'

Love Is The Master

Of All That We Dream

Plantin' The Seeds

That We Reap

Love We Conceive

From Things Unseen

A Reality

Of Our Own Makin'

So How Did You Know

That You Didn't Know

Where Did You Get

That Information From

The Whole Of U're Mind

Body An' Soul

Begins To Arise

U're Spirit Is Ascendin'. ☆

HUMBLE

♣♠♣

Were Not Yet Nearly
    Were Hardly An' Barely
        On Part Of The Journey
            That Were Yet To Take

Beyond The Confusion
    Its' Only Illusions
        Born Of Delusions
            As We Take Our First Steps

Faith To The Faithless
    Is Stranger Than Strangers
        Away From The Danger
            You Might Find U're Way

Its' Hard To Believe It
    Sometimes You Feel It
        Even If You Can't See It
        Along The Way

Its' Not Really Far Now
    But Closer Than Somehow
        In Time We Might Find Out
        The Reasons Why

Whatever It Could Be
Wherever It Might Be
However We Might Dream
Until We Wake Up

Even Though The Humble
Might Stumble
The Laws Of The Jungle
Dictates Our Fate

An' Even If Victories Crumble
There's So Much To Reap
Before The End Of The Day. ☆

REVENGE
♧♤♧

Hell Hath No Fury Except To Be Scorned
I Guess You Were Born With A Bone To Pick

A Pound Of Flesh To Pay Off Our Debts
But Its' Hard To Caress An' Ego Deflated

The Higha' The Stakes, The Harda' The Breaks
For Those Who Want Somethin' For Nuthin'

Even Jokers An' Fools Who Break All The Rules
Know That True Love Is All That They Wanted

Funny How Shame Turned Into Blame
As We Live With The Pain Of The Consequences

But Right From The Start We All Played The Part
To Renda' Our Hearts Instead Of Our Garments

After Goodbye We Live With The Lie
That One That Denied Us Any Justice

Addiction Is Not Jus' A Drug
An' No Amount Of Money Can Buy You Love

An' Yet These Crimes Of Passion Lead Us To Redemption
So Take U're Revenge For U're Satisfaction. ☆

SOUL SACRED SACRIFICE
(THE WORLDS FOUNDATIONS)

Life Is Long, Time Is Longer

A Passin' Thought

But Jus' Let It Linger

21 Or 33, 3x7 An' That's Jus' Poetry

So Before You Roll The Dice

You Betta' Think About It Twice

With The Soul Sacred Sacrifice

We Can Rock The Worlds Foundations

You Can't Fool A Fool

Without Intelligence

So How Do You Know

When Someone's

Talkin' Nonsense

Before The Common Era

Before The Days Of A.D

Well We Was Gettin' Prepared

For What Might Be

So If You Need Some Good Advice

Somebody True Who Can Provide

For The Soul Sacred Sacrifice

We Can Rock The Worlds Foundations

If Only We Could

Dream The Same Dream

Without Any Bias In-Between

Coz Lightning Never Strikes

In The Same Place Twice

But If It Ever Did

It Might Cause A Sensation

For All The Stars Up In The Sky

Might Hold The Keys To Paradise

For The Soul Sacred Sacrifice

We Can Rock The Worlds Foundations. ☆

SAMSONITE

♣♠♣

Sometimes Its' Hard
To See The World
The Way That It Is
When U're Lookin' At It
Through A Lens

U're So Uninspired
By All The Curves An' Lines
As U're Blinded By The Things
Flyin' In The Sky

It Seems That You Prefer
In Stickin' To U're Lies
An' All The Things
That They Describe

I Was Only Lookin'
For A Little While
I Was Only Distracted
For A Moment In Time

I Know Its' Not A Fair Fight
But U've Thrown The Gauntlet Down
An' Now This Coward
Has To Stand His Ground

Trapped Beside The Pillars
The Free Will Of Religions
Where The Gargoyles An' Demons
Have Battles Of Their Own

Picture A Movie Scene
Here Comes Reality
I've Got The Strength Of A Samsonite
But I'm Feelin' Weak

Without A Name For God
They'll Explain It Away
An' Replace It All
With A Fairytale. ☆

I NEVER COULD

If Tomorrow Sorrows Never Ends'
Will Misery Keep Me Company

If I Was Made To Break U're Heart
Jus' To Prove I Could Make You Happy

If Loneliness Is Jus' A Part
Of Gettin' Closer To The Truth

If Sadness Takes My Tears Away
As I Yearn To Get Closer To You

If All This Cryin' An' Fear Of Dyin'
Bears The Pain I've Lived Through

An' If This Decimation Of Our Destruction
Is Jus' The Resurrection Of A Promise Renewed

If All This Waitin' In Isolation
Is Jus' The Commitments Of A Fool

If All This Prayin' In Meditation
Carries The Hopes, I Never Could. ☆

HOME
♣♠♣

You Know That Railway Track

Ain't Gonna Take You Back

Somewhere Down The Line

To Where Its' At

Its' Jus' An' Infinite Circle

That's Incomplete

Funny How The Past

Has Fallen At U're Feet

You Think That Time Machine

Full Of Wishes An' Dreams

Is Gonna Make You Feel

Contented An' Happy

Well All We Ever Do

Is Wish Upon A Star

Funny How That Star

Has Fallen Too Far

Everythin' That You Have

Everythin' That You Own

Everythin' That You Want Is Long Gone

Now That U've

Pulled Ya' Boot Straps

All By U'reself

Funny How U've Fallen

For Everythin' Else

Ain't No Mexican Gringo

From The High Chaparral

Ain't No Dukes Of Hazard

Tearin' Up This Town

Ridin' For U're Freedom

Alias' Smith An' Jones

No Little House On The Prairie

To Make You Feel At Home. ☆

THE COMPASSIONATE ONE
♣♤♣

Though A Man In Prison, May Have Sealed His Fate
Still He Hears A Voice, When The Music Is Played

Could It Be The Sound Of Joy An' Peace
To One Day Learn, He May Be Set Free

Somehow Those Citizens Of Planet Earth
Who's Only Reward Is To Be Born Again

Though Some May Never See
Who Really Holds The Key, To A Paradise Of Eternity

Is There Such A Thing As Life After Death
Could It Be A Belief, Or A Myth To Regret

When Its' So Hard To Forget This Material Life
A Lifetime In Heaven, A Freedom Never Denied

Why The Compassionate One, Even Took The Time
To Forgive Mankind, For His Most Heinous Crimes

Well Its' So Hard To Fathom, The Trials Of This Life
Or Could It Be Resistance Is Futile. ☆

YOU AN' I

Now That U're Leavin'
Its' A Strange An' Funny Feelin'

Its' Kinda' Hard To Know
How You Feel Inside

Even Though We Were Never Married
Its' Kinda' Harder To Carry

The Weight Of This Dream
Is Heavy On My Mind

Now The End Of This Game
Is Leavin' No One To Blame

Like A Moth To The Flame
We Both Got Burned

An' Now Its' Fallen Apart
Pieces Of Broken Hearts

Coz We Both Played The Part
Lovers Like To Play

Now That The Passion Had Passed
I Think You Know Me At Last

I Guess You Figured Out
Were Gettin" Nowhere

Whatever U're Lookin' For
I Guess You Gotta' Explore

I Guess That Open Door
Was Callin' U're Name

I Guess You An' I
We're Kinda' Stuck

Much Before The Time
We Ever Broke Up

I Guess You An' I
Jus' Ran Out Of Luck

An' Its' So Hard To Start Again
An' Its' So Hard To Give You Up. ☆

A JEALOUS GOD

For What Interferes, Intervenes
An' Now There's Somethin' Tearin' At The Seams

A Reality Of Modern Dreams
A Concept Made Of Esoteric Things

Its' Hard To Imagine, But What Would You Do
If A Portion Of This Truth Was Handed Over To You

In Spite Of This Spite, We Imitate The Light
Jus' Like A Fallen Angel In Disguise

As All Of Things Begin To Fade
By The End Of The Day, The Decades In Decay

For What Love Desires We Long To Acquire
As We Covet The Prize Through A Deception Of Lies

A Jealous God Has Somehow Lost
All Of Such Things He Had Created

An' Yet It Never Seems To Be Enough
To Keep Us Satisfied, To Keep Us Forever Grateful. ☆

TRUTH

♣♠♣

A Force Of Nature Is A Tour De' Force

As The Wheels Of Chance An' The Turbines Are Turnin'

An' Earthquake Murmurs' An' The Stars Crash Down

With A Compass To Navigate For Mappin' The Ground

A River Meanders Through The Desert Sands

An' The Clouds Are Sailin' Like A Caravan

A Burnin Oasis Of Forgotten Lands

From The Whisperin' Of U're Masterplan

A Thought Transcends The Meta-Physical

An' Abstract Mind Will Always Do That To You

In The Reality Of Esoteric Subsistence

In A Perfect World Without No Resistance

She Must Have Got The Good News

She Must Have Read All The Reviews

She Must Have Got The Cryptic Clues

She Must Have Found The Secrets

Revealin' The Truth. ☆

3 DIMENSIONAL

Once We Arrive

As The Terminal Of Life

Inside The Departure Lounge

Beyond This Twilight Zone

That Governs An' Controls

Searchin' For Our Freedoms

Tryin' To Make It Home

As Waterfalls Of Baptism

Rain Down On Us All

An' Paradise Is A Place

We Were Waitin' For

To Wash Away All The Remnants

To Remove All The Stains

All The Heartache An' Torments

The Sufferin' An' Pain

For U're Soul To Evolve

Why Should You Have To Crawl

Now That U're Standin' Tall

They Call It Emancipation

Risin' Up From The Depths

To Be Born Again

Way Beyond All Realms

Of Possibilities

Jus' As U're Spirit

Is Beginnin' To Climb

Somewhere Out Of Body

But Not Out Of Mind

Toward The Seventh Heaven

In The Sky

A 3 Dimensional Being

In Jus' Beginnin' To Dream. ☆

GOD'S BABY

Complicated Wasn't Naked
Now There's Nuthin' Left To Hide Behind

Somethin' Jilted Might Be Jaded
Until Those Stains Are Washed Away

Anotha' Day On U're Way To Heaven
Anotha' Night In Paradise

U're Hopes An' Prayers Of Promises
Anotha' Light That's Beginning To Shine

Sincerity Is Full Of Sweetness
But Honesty Is Cruel To Be Kind

For Every Night That Fills You With Moonlight
For Every Day Like The Sun You Will Rise

Maybe God's Baby Could Explain It
Somethin' So Simple To Hard To Comprehend

An' All The While We Try To Redeem It
Someone Of Value, Someone To Set Us Free. ☆

UNAFFECTED

♣♠♣

I Fear The Worst Is Grave

Can Mankind Still Be Saved

To Free Him From Himself

If He Has No Fear Of Nothin'

Its' Jus' A Matta' Of Time

Til' Were Raptured From The Vine

Or Somethin' So Divine

The Wise Man Was Sayin'

The Black Sheep That Strayed

Far Away From The Flock

Is Risin' Up An' Ascendin'

From The Unorthodox

Of A Netherworld

Far Beyond The Gates

Of Our Ruins

In This Wilderness

We're Facin' The Wild West

But Truly We Are Blessed

With So Much Courage

Until From Whence It Came

You Heard Him Call Out Ya' Name

An' Now The Shepherd Waits

As You Pay U're Homage

As I Contain My Thoughts

I'm Reconnectin'

As I Contain My Soul

I'm Redirected

As I Contain My Heart

It Comes Unexpected

As I Contain My Spirit

I'm Still Unaffected. ☆

JIBBA JABBA BIRD

♧♤♧

Everybody's Waiting For An' Age
But It Takes A Long Time To Turn The Page

What's Written In The Past Seems To Reoccur
It Could Be A Nightmare Or A Dream Deferred

Somehow Humanity Has Lost The Will To Seek
A Voice Of Unity Of Which We Use To Speak

An' Happiness Is The Faintest Sound
As History's Heartbeat Echoes Underground

An' Some May Say The Beauty Of Decay
Is Like A Crucifixion In The Bed We Lay

For All The Faith We Had Why Did We Turn Away
An' Turn To The Objects That We've Learnt To Hate

An' Those Prophetic Words
Of The Jibba' Jabba' Bird

Could Be Mankind's Extinction
That We've Come To Observe

For What Happens Now May Not Be Of Concern
But Its' Imminent Now, For The Jibba' Jabba' Bird. ☆

PRAY TODAY

♣♠♣

Now I'm Workin' On Borrowed Time

But You Can Say Its' All On Faith

There's No Other Reasons To Be Justified

I Guess You Can Say Its' All By Grace

There's No Pretendin' Why My World Is Endin'

As I'm Contendin' With The Truth

An' All The Reasons For My Belief

Is Somethin' That I Found In You

Anotha' Life, Or Anotha' Time

Anotha' Reason To Search My Soul

Where Do We Go, Well I'll Never Know

My Only Hope Is To Make It Home

So Could It Be My Fuel For Thought

As My Imagination Runs Away

Could It Be A Clash Of Minds

Or The Reasons Why, I Got To Pray Today. ☆

FALLEN

♧♤♧

As The Weapons You Forge Are Used Against Me
As U're Inquisition Interrogates Me

As You Seem To Want To Gag An' Bind Me
Before You Nail An' Crucify Me

It Seems You Won't Be Satisfied
Until I Finally Gone Out Of My Mind

From The Tortured Cries Of A Primal Screamin'
An' All The Fears My Soul Is Feelin'

Incessantly An' Deeply Tormented
It Seems These Demons Are Demented

While Breakin' Down My Natural Defences
Invadin' Into All Of My Spaces

As My Boundaries Are Disrespected
With U're Disdain Full Of Hatred

From All The Anger That U're Ventin'
Now That This Muse Is Condescendin'

So Jus' How Strong Do You Want Me To Be
Before I've Finally Fallen On My Knees. ☆

CITY OF ZENN

I Hear That Heaven

Is A City Of Zenn

An' If U've Bein' There Before

U'll Go There Again

The Say Its' A Place

Of Joy An' Happiness

An' Overwhelmin' Feelin'

That You Can't Forget

They Say There's No Excuse

To Replace What Is True

But In The City Of Zenn

U're Irreplaceable

So Whatever You Say

There's Nothin' In The Way

Cos Everyday's A New Day

In The City Of Zenn

Well Some Are Makin' Hay

By The Light Of The Day

An' Some Are Makin' Plans

Before The Moonlight Fades

Well I Think That My Prayer

Was Answered Today

As I Made My Way

Into The City Of Zenn

An If You Look Deep Inside

Somewhere Within'

They Say Its' A Journey

To A Place Without End

An' When You Arrive

You Can Walk Right In

Cos Everybody's Welcome

To The City Of Zenn. ☆

AN ODE' TO GOD

As I Lean Upon My Own Intention
As I Bear The Weight Of My Own Invention

I Hardly Knew How Much I Was Lost
Until I Came Upon The Cross

Through The Endless Thoughts Of My Meditation
Through The Ministry Of My Imagination

I Wandered Through Places I've Never Known
If Only To Find My Way Back Home

Through The Blessedness An' The Gifts That You Bring
Surely Swiftly Flies, Like A Bird On The Wind

For The Countless Things, That I Must Behold
You Are The One, The One I Am Told

Now I Follow A Path, Of Which I'm Not Certain
Now I Sind You This Song, An' Ode' To Love

Now I Follow The Roads, Searchin' For Heaven
Now That I Know, Its' An' Ode' To God. ☆

ETERNAL LIFE

♣♤♣

Judgin' By The Cover

Of That Lonesome Book

Seems That I Bein'

Undervalued An' Overlooked

But They Say Once You Know

How The Story Goes

Its' Always Upto You

How You Walk That Road

An' So The Autumn Leaves

Turn From Brass To Gold

Upon The Lazy Bones

Of An' Aging Soul

Still I'm Siftin' Through Words

To Find Some Inspiration

Somethin' That I Learned

Jus' For This Occasion

Maybe U've Had Enough

Maybe U've Had Too Much

What U're Expectin' To Change

Is Jus' The Same Ole' Stuff

They Say It Goes In Circles

They Say Its' Comin' Aroun'

With One Foot In The Grave

An' Ure Head In The Clouds

Cos I Bein' Runnin' This Race

Still Wonderin' Why

If Its' All Jus' Bein'

A Waste Of Time

That Unspoken Contract

Of Do Or Die

Jus' To Reach That Prize

Of Eternal Life ☆

INVOCATIONS

♣♠♣

Entreaty Angelus Domini, Wu Tou Mi Tao
Dao Li Chi Sun Li, Esprit De Core De Spirit
Le Tissu De La Vie, L'amour De La Vie
Pa Hsien, Tsao Chen, Men Shen, Cheng Huang, Fuxing
Pusa, Inshallah, Amenominakanushinokami
Ai Dao De Jing, Ai Lubaoshi, I In Love, Uck Han Dudullud

አንጀለስ ዶሚኒ፤ ዉ ቱ ሚ ታኦ፤ ዳኦ ሊ ቺ ሱን ሊ፤ እስፐሪት ዴ ኮር ዴ
ስፐሪት፤ ሌ ቲሱ ዴ ላ ቪዬ፤ ላሞር ዴ ላ ቪዬ፤ ፓ ሂየን፤ ፃኦ ቼን፤ መን ሼን፤
ቼንግ ሁኣንግ፤ ፉክስንግ፤ ፑሳ፤ ኢንሻላህ፤ አሚኖሚናካኑሺኖካሚ፤ አይ ዳኦ ዴ
ጂንግ አይ ሉባኦሺ፤ እኔ በፍቅር፤ ኡክ ሃን ዱዱሉድ።

याचनाएन्जेलस डोमिनी, वू तौ मी ताओ, दाओ ली ची सन ली
एसपरिट दे कोर दे सुपरिटि, ले टसिसु दे ला विए, ल'अमूर दे ला
विए पा हसिएन, त्साओ चेन, पुरुष शेन, चेंग हुआंग, फक्सगि, पुसा
इन्शाल्लाह, अमेनोमनिकानुशनिोकामी, ऐ दाओ दे जगि ऐ
लुबाओशी, आई इन लव, उक हान दुदुल्लुड. ☆

· 312 ·

LAST TEMPTATION

My Last Temptation Was You

An' Everythin' I Thought I Knew

Somethin' Like Black Magic

Or Somethin' Like Voodoo

Or Somethin' Hypnotic

From A Witches Brew

My Last Temptation Was A Sin

An' It Almost Broke Me From Within

I Guess I Gambled Now An' Then

I Guess I Took A Risk On All Or Nothin'

My Last Temptation Was Only A Dream

Between What I Want An' What I Need

A Compromise Of The Heart

Until I Fell Apart Right At The Seams

Until My Dreams Were Nothin'

My Last Temptation In My Life

Was What Would Happen If I Died

Would I See Paradise

From The Look In U're Eyes

Or Would I Somehow Forfeit

For What I've Sacrifice.☆

THE HIGHEST BIDDA'

The Victim Perpetrates A Fraud

An' Now U're In Too Deep

An' You Can't Get Out

For An' Ounce Of Gold

You Wanna Be Richa'

The Gatekeepa' Knows

The Winna' Takes It All

A Triple Double Cross

An' Now U're Out In The Cold

For What Doesn't Kill You

Only Makes You Stronga'

So You Sold U're Soul

To The Highest Bidda'.☆

TODAY
(BEG, STEAL AN' BORROW)

♣♤♣

As Much As We

Like To Run Aroun'

It Always Seems That Time

Is Runnin' Out

As Much As We Inherit

We've Squandered This Peace

Jus' For Somethin' Else

That We're Hopin' To See

As Much As We

Yearn To Be Free

Still We're All Indentured

Jus' Like Slaves

A Fool Will Lend You His Knowledge

For Somethin' In Return

An' Yet This Is A Lesson

That We Mus' Learn

As For Every Portion

Now That U're Stakin' U're Claim

Now That U're Bread Is Buttered

For All The Pieces You Break

Still We're Destined To Suffer

For All The Progress We Make

Coz All The Problems We Face

Are All Man Made

An' So We Beg Steal An' Borrow

From Yesterday

With All Of The Talents

That We've Ever Made

But Don't You Know That Tomorrow

Will Make You Pay

For All Of The Love

That You Need Today.☆

TOMORROW

♧♤♧

Well Ain't It Funny

How Our Lives Turned Out

Jus' To Think Back Then

We Thought We Figured It Out

When All The Choices We Made

Have Led Us To Right Now

If Only We Knew Then

What It Was All About

Now You Can Fall In Line

Or You Can Fall Apart

An' You Can Take U're Time

But Jus' Don't Take Too Much

Jus' Like The Early Bird

Might Be A Second Too Late

Before You Break The Record

Let's Set The Record Straight

Before It All Back Fires

It Might Fire Back

Before You Start Changin' Lanes

Make Sure U're Right On Track

Before You Second Guess

You Betta' Know The Rest

You Got To Know The Theory

Before You Take The Test

Now Its' Easy Come An' Easy Go

I Guess You Never Know Until You Know

It Could Be Here Today

But Its' Gone Tomorrow

Now That You Know For Sure

Tomorrow Never Comes.☆

GOOD DEEDS

♧♤♧

As For All The Good That We've Done
Still You Remain The Lonely One
For All The Charity That You Do
Still Doesn't Prove That U'll Be Excused

So How Could They Know What's Inside Of U're Head
Was There Ever A Reason To Be Afraid
From The Very Moment That We Strayed
These Accursed Rituals Were Already Made

As For The Enmity Between You An' Me
As For Why Thy Seed Has Bruise Thy Heal
As For Every Child From Each An' Every Tribe
Has Only Jus' Arrived In Time To See The Signs

Well Now Here's A Passage Between Old Friends
Who May Never Pass By This Way Again
For The Remainin' Days Of Our Lives
Is All That We Have Left For Us To Reconcile

Jus' Like A Slave Turnin' The Page
While Darin' To Tempt The End Of Days
Takin' Delight From All U're Good Deeds
But It Seems That U're Fate Was Already Sealed.☆

MARY JANE
(ANOMALIES)

♣♠♣

Have You Seen Mary Jane

Since She Changed Her Name

Now She's Lois Lane

In Some Other Movie

Those Angels Up Above

Have All Fallen In Love

I've Seen Em' One By One

Slippin' An' Slidin'

Have You Seen Mary Jane

Since She Changed Her Name

Now That The Fortune An' Fame

Has Made Her So Famous

The Girl Behind The Bar

Mus' Be A Tinsel Star

They Picked Her Up In A Car

Driven By A Chauffer

The Girl I Loved Before

Went Walkin' Out The Door

Now I'm Turnin' The Page

To Begin A Chapter

An' All Those Lovers Like Me

Who Keep On Payin' A Fee

To A Datin' Agency

Lookin' For Perfection

Have You Seen Mary Jane

Since She Changed Her Name

Now That She's Hooked On Cocaine

Its' In The Mornin' Papers

The World Is Goin' Insane

An' We're The Ones To Blame

I Wonda' What Will Remain

When Its' All Over

Somewhere On Capitol Hill

They're All Expressin' Their Will

But Its' Jus' Anotha' Thrill

In The U.S Of A

Still Its' The Same Over Here

Placards In Parliament Square

I Wonda' If They Care

Whose Really Protestin'

My Daddy Died Before

The End Of The Last War

The One I'm Fightin' For

Me An' Mary Jane

Here's Some Anomalies

I Found Em' In The Street

I Saved A Couple For Me

An' Gave Some To My Neighbour

Those Idiosyncrasies

Is Somethin' That I Might Need

I'll Give You Some For Free

If You Do Me A Favour.☆

COULDN'T SATISFY

♧♤♧

What's The Point Of Livin'
    Trippin' On This Lie

        What's The Point Of Fightin'
         Tryin' To Survive

A Thief Will Catch A Thief
    A Spy Will Catch A Spy

        But Why Send Us The Devil
           If U're Love Couldn't Satisfy

What's The Point Of Talkin'
    If No Ones Listenin'

        An' What's The Point Of Hopin'
         If Its' Only Wishful Thinkin'

Like Those Angels An' Demons
    Are Bound To Fall An' Rise

        But Why Send Us The Devil
           If U're Love Couldn't Satisfy

What's The Point Of Dreams
　　If They're Never Realized

　　　　An' What's The Point Of Being Good
　　　　If You Only See The Bad Side

We Could Be Cops Or Robbers
　　The Righteous Or Unjustified

　　　　But Why Send Us The Devil
　　　　　If U're Love Couldn't Satisfy

You Could Send Us A Prophet
　　You Could Make Us A Saint

　　　　You Could Give Us The Wisdom
　　　　　For All The Pictures We Paint

For Everything That We Build
　　For All That We Sacrifice

　　　　But Why Send Us The Devil
　　　　　If U're Love Couldn't Satisfy.☆

JUS' CAN'T FIND YOU

♣♠♣

I Bein' Way Out There

Searchin' Everywhere

Sometimes I Stop An' Stare

But I Jus' Can't Find You

I Bein' Way Up Town

Bein' Lookin' All Aroun'

Sometimes I'm Inside Out

But I Jus' Can't Find You

I Bein' Every Place

Bein' Dreamin' Of U're Face

Hopin' To Find A Trace

But I Jus' Can't Find You

Sometimes I'm In A Crowd

Still Hopin' That U'll Be Found

But As I Look Aroun'

I Jus' Can't Find You

I've Walked In Every Bar

An' Wondered Where You Are

I've Wished On Every Star

But I Jus' Can't Find You

Sometimes I Get So Scared

An' Its' The Sum Of All My Fears

As I'm Reduced To Tears

But I Jus' Can't Find You

How Can A Jealous Love

Demand My Affections

Why Does Somebody Else

Want My Attention

What Is This Vanity

Hopin' To Prove

While U're Lookin' At Him

While I'm Lookin' At You.☆

DISAPPOINTMENTS

♣♤♣

Fully Equipped
    With All Of The Remnants
        Avoidin' Causalities
            Of U're Own Disaster
                Facin' The Mirror
                    Concealin' The Judgements

Watchin' Humanity
    While Imitatin' The Sun
        A Neurotic Mind
            Chaotic Reverberation
                Slowly Emergin' From
                    The Depths Of A Black Hole
From Now Fearin'
    All Of The Worst
        An' Yet To Believe In
            All Of The Foremost
                Anotha' Egotistical Socialite
                Lickin' The Wounds
                Still Their
                    Somewhat Oblivious

From Anotha' Crack
    A Chink In The Armour
        From The Savin' Grace
            Of The Adorin' Heroine
                I Know That U've Got
                    All Of The Answers

But Why Don't You
    Watch U're Mouth
        Before Those
            Defeated Disappointments
            Come Aroun'
                An' Shut You Down.☆

EVERYONE'S SOUL

♣♤♣

It Seems The Protected

Have Become The Rejected

Now That The Shoe

Is On The Other Foot

It Seems That The Chosen

Forever Now Are Frozen

It Jus' Doesn't Fit

Not Even One Bit

Still We Queue Up

An' Line Up

Jus' To Be First

For All The Lessons We Learn

Of Blessin's An' Curse

An' Who's In Front Of You

An' Who's In Front Of Me

An' What Hangs In The Balance

In The Face Of Adversity

Still The

Compassionate Nature

Of A Holy Soul

Has Now Become Somethin'

We Can Hardly Afford

An' Yet These Victims We See

Scattered On The Streets

Are Cryin' Out For Love

For Somethin' To Eat

Yet The Story Of God

Is Always Told

Somewhere In The Shadows

It Echoes An' Blows

Still The Wind Never Changes

The Direction It Goes

The Truth Will Be Known

In Everyone's Soul.☆

I KNOW
(WE'RE ONLY HUMAN)
♧♤♧

I Know You Wanna See Me

Make A Mistake

Jus' So You Can Accuse Me

Of My Wrong Doing

I Know You Wanna See

My Spirit Break

Jus' So You Can Bring Me

To My Own Ruin

I Know You Wanna See

If I Hesitate

So You Can Twist An' Turn

All Of The Screws In

I Know You Wanna See

If I'm Afraid

Jus' To Keep Me

Locked Down

In My Confusion

I Know You Wanna See Me

Walk Away

Or Simply Watch Me Squirm

In Desperation

I Know You Wanna See

If I'm A Fake

Or Even Try To Shame Me

In My Humiliation

If It Wasn't For Love

I Wouldn't Stay

Coz We Both Know

Its' Jus' An Illusion

Or Could It Be

We're All The Same

So Why Can't You See

We're Only Human.☆

A STATE OF GRACE

♣♤♣

If Chivalry Is Not Dead

Then Tell Me Why Is Romance Dyin'

With Every Heartbeat That I Take

Nuthin' Can Stop

All These Tears That I'm Cryin'

All Of My Life

I've Bein' Searchin' To Find

Until The Day That I Found You

But For Now It Seems

The Gods Are Against Me

When I Try To Prove

That My Love Is True

Whenever The Thought

Enters My Mind

Somethin' Like A Dream

Begins To Arrive

Jus' As I'm Feelin'

Contented An' So Satisfied

A State Of Grace

Begins To Subside

You Know I Love You Mo'

Than Words Can Ever Say

An' Yet Its' Always The Words

That Gets In The Way

An' Why Must It Always Be My Fate

That I Should Lose You

In A State Of Grace. ☆

MY LIFE

♣♠♣

I'm Gonna Take My Time
To Get What's Mine

I'm Gonna Stand In Line
I'm Gonna Do What's Right

I Paid My Dues
An' I'm Nobody's Fool

An' I Done My Best
To Follow The Rules

I'm Gonna Raise My Voice
I'm Gonna Make A Noise

But I Won't Make A Fuss
If You Give Me A Choice

I'm Gonna Do My Thing
However It Swings

Its' Jus' The Way That I Am
Its' Jus' The Way That I'm Livin'

I Don't Wanna Be Standin' Still
I Don't Wanna Trip On Anotha' Pill

I Don't Wanna Be On My Own
But I'll Go It Alone, Whenever I Have Too

I'm Gonna Have To Take Care
I'm Gonna Take It Right There

It Could Be My Last Chance
I Got To Be Prepared

Don't Wanna Pass It By
I Got To Keep It in Sight

An' Maybe One Day
You Might Be Besides Me

Either Way, If U're Gonna Hate
Whatever I Do, You Hold It Against Me

Either Way, However It Takes Me
I'm Gonna Live My Life, An' It Starts Tonight. ☆

THE SAME

♣♤♣

If Only For Today

Everybody Is The Same

If Only For One Day

Everybody Is The Same

Its' The Same Highs

Its' The Same Lows

Its' The Same Pain

Its' The Same Blues

Could Be Somethin' So Random

Keepin' Us In Tandem

With All This Unity

Its' Funny How It Found Us

Keepin' Us In Balance

With Synchronicity

If Only Today

Everybody Is The Same

In Their Own Natural Way

Everybody Is The Same

Its' The Same Sky

Its' A Rainbow

Its' The Same Clouds

Its' The Same Snow

It Could Be Someone Attractive

Starts To Fill You With Magic

That Makes It So Surreal

There Could Be Somethin' Contagious

As We're Passin' As Strangers

Now We Got Synergy

If Only For Today

Everybody Is The Same

No Matta' How We Change

Everybody Is The Same

Its' The Same Wants

Its' The Same Needs

Its' The Same Dreams

The Same Fantasies

How Could The Duality

Begin A Rhythm An' Beat

An' Call It Harmony

The Suddenly You An' Me

Are Caught Up Subconsciously

On A Brand New Scene. ☆

BREAK FREE

This Rejection

Was For U're Protection

The Mo' I Wanted You

The Mo' They Turned Against Me

I Know This Love

Was Always Too Much

Suffocatin' You

An' Overpowerin' Me

Givin' Up, I Didn't Wanna Stop

Even Though It Was Fun

It Was Hurtin' Me

Though Its' All In Vain

I Know You Couldn't Stay

But It Was Always

Because Of The Others

You Push Me Away

So Where Do You Go

If No Means No

Blowin' Hot An' Blowin' Cold

Provocatively

An' All These Flirtations

Of Infatuations

Well It Was You Or Them

All B'coz Of Me

An' The Same Air

Was Harda' To Breathe

The Touch Of U're Body

The Feel Of U're Heartbeat

Still I Wanted You

As I Suffered Defeat

The Mo' I Tasted You

The Mo' I Couldn't

Break Free. ☆

BIRTHDAY SUIT

If Only I Could See

Past U're Eyes

Deep Inside U're Soul

Where You Fantasize

Don't Push Me Away

You Know What I'm Here For

Why Don't You Let Me Inside

An' Jus Close The Door

An' So The Crucifixion Begins

A Love Addiction

When It Was Always Written

In U're Heart

I Know Its' Hard To Believe

Beyond A Lovers Dream

When The World Aroun' Us

Is Goin' Stir Crazy

I Know The Disappointed

Always Knew What They Wanted

An' They Would Do Anythin'

To Make It Come True

An' Every Night They've Bein' Waitin'

To Break Their Ultimatums

If Someone Made Them An' Offer

They Couldn't Refuse

A Million Miles An' A Million Trials

Through The Highs An' The Lows

Searchin' For You

A Million Years An' A Million Tears

Til I Saw You Standin' Their

In U're Birthday Suit

Til I Saw You Standin' There

Kinda Filthy Cute

Til I Saw You Standin' There

In The Light Of The Truth. ☆

CITIZENS OF PLANET EARTH
(SECOND BIRTH)

Father Time Was Punchin' The Clock
Watchin' As The Days We're Tickin' Away
Mother Nature Was Plantin' Seeds In Her Garden
Prayin' Everyday For Sunshine An' Rain

From All Of The People You Could Ever Meet
They're All Livin' Here Right Down On This Street
An' Yet We Never Greet A Single Soul
Until Somebody Stops An' Says Hello

I Guess We're Only Here To Make A Connection
Until We Harmonise An' Make The Same Reflections
Until We Open Up Mind, Body An' Soul
Until We're All Aligned An' Ready To Move On

If You Don't Know What U're Life Is Worth
U're One Day Away From A Second Birth
Until That Day When The Lessons Are Learnt
You Know We're Only Citizens Of Planet Earth. ☆

MO' THAN MAGIC

♣♤♣

The Other Day

You Called My Name

From A Place Faraway

I Was Strayin'

An' All This Time

Inside Of My Mind

I Didn't Realize

I Was Lamentin'

The Watchmen Who Seek

What Could Be

A Witness Participatin'

Somehow I Knew

The Promise Of You

The Signs Had Indicated

The Greatest Piece

Of My Portion

Of My Life

I Dedicate It

Besides The Seeds

That I Sow

The Body Of My Temple

For The Faith In Me

What I Believe

Blinded Me

Jus' Like Magic

But The Work Of U're Hands

Made Me Understand

This Miracle's

Mo' Than Magic. ☆

EBENEZER'S STONE
(GHOST OF CHRISTMAS)

The Ghost Of Christmas Past Comes A' Creepin'
Hauntin' Me By My Bed, As I'm Sleepin'

Somewhere In A Dream, I'm Wide Awake
As He's Warnin' Me, About To Seal My Fate

The Ghost Of Christmas Present Is Desperately Waitin'
Warnin' Me Of Mistakes, That I've Bein' Makin'

Outside My Window, Tappin' At The Door
As I'm Goin' Insane, He's Tellin' Me To Change

The Ghost Of Christmas Future Is Jus' Arrivin'
Bringin' Me Some Hope, On The Horizon

It Seems My Redemption Is At Hand
In What Appears To Be A Second Chance

Somehow I Know I Can't Do It Alone
Not Without The Help Of Ebenezer's Stone

As Much As I May Need To Atone
Its' Somethin' I Mus' Face All On My Own. ☆

HEAVEN
♧♤♧

How Can We Know

This Place Of Abode

Is High Above The Shadows,

Within The Clouds

As Much As We're Born For

We Live An' Cry For

A Place Within This Paradise

Since The Beginnin'

We We're Forgiven

After Livin' With The Hopes

Our Sins Would Be Washed Away

For As Much As We Want Too

Simply Jus' Walk Through

The Halls An' Corridors Of Hallelujah

For The Procession That Sings

Of Heavenly Things

For The Saints An' Prophets,

For The Martyrs Departed

As Much As We May

Turn Every Page

With Feet Of Sand Clay

Still We Pray

Like The Faithful Hearted

Cos' In This Previous Life

Love Was Crucified

Awaitin' To Arise

In A Beautiful Heaven

An' So We Hope To Resides

After Livin' This Life

To One Day Arrive

In This Beautiful Heaven. ☆

ONE DAY A WEEK
(A THOUSAND YEARS)

♧♤♧

GENESIS:

SUN: 1, 400

MON: 2, 500

TUE: 3, 600

WED: 4, 700

THU: 5, 800

FRI: 6, 900

SAT: 7, 000

REVELATION: ☆

PURPORTED
(Angel-Trans-Lation)

So It Is
Uck-Han-Dudullud
I Declare It Is So
Dudullud-Uck-Han.♡

A Kentɛmplatıv ˈƏʊd

♫ ♪ Tʊ Ðə ˈTʃif Muzishan ♪ ♩

A Tao.House Product / THE JIBBA JABBA BIRD
JUFUREH NIUMI IYAHMAHCAH WESTERN INDIANS
Valentine Fountain of Love Ministry
Info contact: **tao.house@live.co.uk**
Copyright: Clive Alando Taylor 2024

Clive Alando Taylor

Printed in the United States
by Baker & Taylor Publisher Services